FRIEDRICH SCHILLER

Born in 1759, Johann Christoph ... first play, *The Robbers* (staged in 1782), while he was a ...... the ducal military academy and then a regimental surgeon in Württemberg. Fleeing from the Duke of Württemberg's displeasure at the play, he accepted a contract from the National Theatre at Mannheim, where he wrote *Fiesco* and *Intrigue and Love* (both staged in 1784) as well as starting *Don Carlos*, which was first performed at Hamburg in 1787.

All of his subsequent plays were staged at the Court Theatre in Weimar, under the direction of his fellow dramatist and poet, Goethe. These included the *Wallenstein* trilogy (1798-99), *Mary Stuart* (1800) and *William Tell* (1804). He was professor of history at Jena from 1789 to 1791 and settled in Weimar in 1799, where he collaborated with Goethe in running the theatre until his death in 1805.

MIKE POULTON

Mike Poulton began writing for the theatre in 1995. His first two productions were staged the following year by the Chichester Festival Theatre: *Uncle Vanya* with Derek Jacobi, and *Fortune's Fool* with Alan Bates. Since then, productions have included *St Erkenwald* at the RSC, *Ghosts* with Nichola McAuliffe at the Theatre Royal Plymouth, *The Dance of Death* and an adaptation of Euripides' *Ion* at the Mercury Theatre Colchester, all directed by David Hunt; *The Three Sisters* with Charles Dance, at the Birmingham Repertory Theatre, directed by Bill Bryden, and *Uncle Vanya* on Broadway with Derek Jacobi, Roger Rees and Laura Linney.

In 2001 his adaptation of the *York Mystery Plays*, directed by Gregory Doran, was performed for the first time in York Minster. In 2003 his *Fortune's Fool*, directed by Arthur Penn on Broadway, received a Tony Award nomination for Best Play, and went on to win seven major awards including the Tony for Best Actor for Alan Bates, and the Tony for Best Featured Actor for Frank Langella. Other commissions include two plays of *The Canterbury Tales*, and two of Mallory's *Morte D'Arthur* for the Royal Shakespeare Company, a new version of Schiller's *Mary Stuart* for Birmingham Repertory Theatre, and a new version of *Gilgamesh*.

Other Classics in Translation

FRIEDRICH SCHILLER

DON
CARLOS

in a new version by
MIKE POULTON

NICK HERN BOOKS
London
www.nickhernbooks.co.uk

A Nick Hern Book

Don Carlos first published in Great Britain as a paperback original in 2005 by Nick Hern Books Limited, 14 Larden Road, London W3 7ST

This translation of *Don Carlos* copyright © 2005 Mike Poulton
Schiller's Don Carlos copyright © 2005 Lesley Sharpe
Introduction copyright © 2005 Mike Poulton

Mike Poulton has asserted his right to be identified as the translator of this work

Cover image: Derek Jacobi in the Sheffield Theatres production of *Don Carlos*, Crucible, 2004. Photographer: Ivan Kyncl

Typeset by Country Setting, Kingsdown, Kent, CT14 8ES
Printed and bound in Great Britain by Cox and Wyman, Reading, Berks

A CIP catalogue record for this book is available from the British Library

ISBN 1 85459 857 0

Contents

Schiller's 'Don Carlos'

by Lesley Sharpe, University of Exeter

'A family portrait in a royal household' – this is how the young playwright Friedrich Schiller (1759-1805) attempted to sell his new project to the Director of the Mannheim National Theatre in 1784. 'A family portrait' sounds cosy but it is a grim scenario that emerges – frustrated and near-incestuous passion, sexual jealousy and intrigue, finally rebellion and murder, all played out within the stifling formalities of court and under the hawk-eyed gaze not only of unscrupulous and self-interested courtiers but also of the Spanish Inquisition. This distinctly uncosy family portrait is painted in Schiller's characteristic dramatic style, through swift-moving action, great set-piece encounters, impassioned speeches and boldly drawn characters. But far from being a domestic tragedy, *Don Carlos* is in fact a wide-ranging historical tragedy that uses a sixteenth-century setting to challenge the political absolutism of the eighteenth.

Don Carlos admittedly offers little in the way of historical fact about the life of the son and heir to Philip II of Spain. Schiller's starting point was not historical source material but a seventeenth-century French bodice-ripper entitled *Dom Carlos. Nouvelle historique* (1672), whose author, the Abbé de Saint-Réal, invented the secret passion between Carlos and Elizabeth. Born in 1545 to his father's first wife, Maria Manuela of Portugal, the historical Carlos showed early signs of mental instability which increased after an accident he had at the age of seventeen. As his paranoia and eccentricity grew more pronounced and he was rumoured to be intending to flee Spain, possibly for Northern Europe, his father took the unprecedented step of having him virtually imprisoned in his room, where he died in 1568 in mysterious circumstances.

In his early phase of work Schiller – himself rather prone in those days to unrequited passion – strongly identified with the unhappy Carlos. Like his hero, the playwright was young and isolated. His first play, *The Robbers*, completed when he was only twenty-one, had been premiered to an enthusiastic audience at the Mannheim National Theatre in 1782 but had brought down on the author, then an army surgeon in Stuttgart, the wrath of his ruling prince, the Duke of Württemberg, who disapproved of its style, its content and of the fact that Schiller had taken French leave to attend a performance in Mannheim in the neighbouring Palatinate. He forbade Schiller to write, and the young playwright took the courageous decision to flee Württemberg and live by his pen. He was planning *Don Carlos* while forced to live incognito and in seclusion on a friend's remote estate to avoid the Duke's spies. Small wonder that Carlos, who longs for sympathy and friendship, caught his imagination. Small wonder that the play's larger, public themes of freedom of conscience and the dignity of the individual, themes central to the European Enlightenment, sprang also from his first-hand experience of the tyranny of Germany's *ancien régime*.

Describing his, as yet unwritten, play as a family portrait was Schiller's tactic to convince the Mannheim theatre that he would cater for contemporary audiences' liking for sentimental dramas of the private sphere. But during his protracted work on the play Schiller immersed himself in the history of the sixteenth century, and though the plot and several key characters, chiefly Rodrigo, are invented, *Don Carlos* offers an interpretation of history, of the sixteenth-century struggle for religious freedom as an anticipation of the eighteenth-century struggle for more liberal and humane government. For Schiller, writing just before the French Revolution, freedom of conscience is an inalienable right. Rodrigo, who daringly professes his beliefs to Philip, is of course a historical anachronism, a man of the Enlightenment whose views echo those of some of the great eighteenth-century thinkers such as Montesquieu and Rousseau. The audience is invited to share with him the confidence that tyranny and the Inquisition will give way to liberty and respect for the individual. But while the play is an affirmation of faith in humanity it is also an exploration of human failings and tragic dilemmas.

Carlos, heir to the most powerful monarch on earth, is a young
man with a great historical mission. He loses sight of it and
rediscovers it only when it is too late. His father is about to
send an army to the Spanish Netherlands to put down the
revolt against his rule and to suppress the Protestant faith. If
Carlos rather than the ruthless Alba can be given the task of
bringing peace and order, then immeasurable bloodshed and
suffering will be prevented. But when Carlos' mentor and
inspiration, Rodrigo, the Marquis of Posa, arrives he finds
Carlos consumed by a hopeless and dangerous passion.
Domingo opens the play by trying to coax the secret out of
Carlos. From that first moment the net is closing around him
and the Queen. Alba and Domingo fear them for the threat they
pose to the old repressive ways:

DOMINGO (*to* ALBA).
    Elizabeth and Carlos were cast in the same mould –
    Reformers, innovators, both over full of zeal.
    They have contracted the same terrible disease: *Humanity*.
    And Humanity, you know, is very contagious.
                          (Act II, Scene 9)

But Carlos' emotional appeal to Philip's fatherly feelings when
he asks to be sent to the Netherlands only provokes contempt
in the aloof monarch. This is not the kind of son he wants. Yet
he suspects that his mistrust of Carlos and later the suspicion
cast on his wife are the result of Alba's and Domingo's
manipulation of him for their own ends. Philip, for all his
coldness, is just beginning to realise that his splendid isolation
is not coupled with god-like omniscience. He desires the trust,
the honesty, the truth that should ideally exist between father
and son, between a powerful ruler and his heir. He seeks a
substitute, a man who looks for no favours and seems to have
the independent judgement Philip needs: Rodrigo.

Rodrigo becomes to Philip the son he wishes he had – proud,
heroic, yet eloquent, diplomatic and a man of principle at the
same time. But the truth that he gives Philip in their central
scene together is the truth not about Carlos and Elizabeth but
about Philip himself and his ruthless politics:

    You wish to plant a garden that will flower for ever.
    Why do you water it with blood?   (Act III, Scene 11)

Philip's persecution of his subjects is not only cruel but futile: 'You can't imprison men's minds.' By seizing the unforeseen moment and challenging the King, Rodrigo is playing an extremely dangerous game. He could be delivered instantly to the Inquisition, but Philip, moved by the younger man's courage and the intensity of his conviction, thinks he has found a potential ally. Rodrigo, who never sought royal favour and uses it to protect Carlos (though Carlos is justifiably confused, as the action progresses, by his friend's seemingly duplicitous actions), is bound to disappoint Philip. Does Rodrigo betray his ideals by becoming an intriguer, as some of his critics have argued? He acts precipitately but he sees the danger threatening Carlos, who is naïve enough to trust Princess Eboli. From Carlos he expects not sentimental but heroic friendship and unswerving trust.

Though Rodrigo gives voice to the play's vision of humanity, it is Philip who is the tour de force of characterisation. The King could have come across simply as a cold-hearted villain, ruthless and vindictive, but Schiller slowly opens up the chink in his armour. He is feared and so he is lonely. He feels his isolation in a court of flatterers and his vulnerability to manipulation by them. He is capable of magnanimity, as his treatment of his defeated Admiral Medina Sidonia illustrates (Schiller brings forward by twenty years the defeat of the Spanish Armada as a sign that Spain's power is waning). He is devastated to discover that on opening his heart a very little, he is betrayed and suffers. And in the penultimate scene with the chilling Cardinal Inquisitor (one of Schiller's great scenes) we see him chastised like a wayward schoolboy and made to relearn his lesson: 'Men – souls – are numbers – no more than that.' Even Philip is ultimately a pawn of the Church.

Don Carlos has a special place in German cultural history. It has always had great resonance in times of oppression. The German liberals of the 1848 Revolution saw themselves as new Rodrigos, pleading for reform with reactionary princes. On a famous occasion in Hamburg in the early years of the Third Reich the audience broke into spontaneous applause at his famous appeal for 'freedom to think and speak' and thus turned the play into a form of protest against the regime. In

1946, when that regime had been overthrown and Germans sought the consolation of their humanist tradition, it was being played in no fewer than twenty-one theatres in Germany. *Don Carlos* is in fact a much more complex and ambiguous work than these stories would suggest. It shows the destruction of the representatives of humanity and the triumph of repression. It also shows how an idealist such as Rodrigo is compromised when he tries to translate ideals into action. In its passionate encounters, vivid characters and intense intelligence and honesty *Don Carlos* shows Schiller at his youthful best.

A Note on the Adaptation

by Mike Poulton

Where I am competent in the language I am to work in, I make my own literal translation before beginning the serious, and lengthy, business of adaptation. In languages where I am not competent – most of them – I commission a literal translation.

I only ever adapt plays I feel passionate about. I've been making notes for this version of *Don Carlos* since studying the play at university, my enthusiasm encouraged for many years by the late Al Woolf, excellent head of German Education at BBC Radio, with whom I worked on a number of projects at Oxford University Press. Michael Grandage commissioned this version from me and allowed me a whole year to cut, fiddle, paste and polish.

Those of you who know the original will remember it as a monster. Even Schiller found his material difficult to control – losing his thread, putting it down, picking it up, repeating himself, misjudging his tone – all this by his own admission: one feels, at times, that he approaches his work armed with a chair and whip, as an animal tamer must approach an undrugged tiger. Schiller's published version would last, I guess, about seven hours. I was faced with the task of bringing it in at under three. I don't believe that the original has ever been performed in its entirety; it wasn't in Schiller's time, and certainly has not been in our own. Productions I have seen of many of Schiller's plays have sometimes seemed like seven hours but have never lasted more than four at the longest.

Given that the original is so lengthy, and contains much repeated philosophy, my method was to use as the skeleton of my version those elements of the play which reveal it as a thriller. After all, we are here – or should be – to please, move, and inspire an audience. The next stage was to lob out any elements of the play that an audience would find absurd because they work against the tone of the majority of the material. For example, in the original, Carlos disguises himself as the ghost of his grandfather, Charles V, in order to terrify the guards who are preventing him from visiting Elizabeth. Don Carlos has been described as Schiller's Hamlet. Certainly Schiller loved all Shakespeare, *Hamlet* especially, and seems to have incorporated many elements of the earlier play in his own. My judgement was that a walking ghost was a step too far – that a modern audience might view it as silliness, and be prompted to laugh out loud at a moment of great sadness. Some characters, too, have been combined, or cut, and their good lines given to others. In these times of hardship in the live theatre in Britain, a cast of forty would make any production financially unattractive. Scenes, or elements of scenes, have been cut or transposed. Modern production calls for pace and flow rather than falling curtains and elaborate changes of setting.

What all this means is that a modern adapter must redesign the architecture of an eighteenth-century play, and make provision for updating its tone, its style, and the method of delivery of its lines, before approaching his work on the words themselves. An adaptation must be accessible, and seem to be in keeping with its period, but avoid jarring modernisms.

Having arrived at a draft, my method is to read it aloud several times, and then to read it aloud with the director – inviting him to challenge anything that seems difficult and obscure. Then I produce a new draft. Next, a cast of actors reads it aloud; I listen and take notes constantly. Then I produce another draft. Finally, throughout the rehearsal period, and during the previews I cut and rewrite, but only a little. I owe a great deal to the excellent cast and director of the first production of *Don Carlos*.

Mike Poulton's version of *Don Carlos* was first performed at the Crucible Theatre, Sheffield, on 22 September 2004, with the following cast:

DOMINGO	Michael Hadley
DON CARLOS	Richard Coyle
RODRIGO, MARQUIS OF POSA	Elliot Cowan
QUEEN ELIZABETH	Claire Price
PRINCESS EBOLI	Charlotte Randle
DUCHESS OF OLIVAREZ	Una Stubbs
GABRIEL DE LA CUEVA	Stuart Burt
KING PHILIP II	Derek Jacobi
DUKE OF ALBA	Ian Hogg
COUNT LERMA	Roger Swaine
DUKE OF MEDINA SIDONIA	Brian Poyser
PRINCE OF PARMA	Paul Keating
COUNT CORDUA	Andrew McDonald
CARDINAL GRAND INQUISITOR	Peter Eyre

Director   Michael Grandage
Designer   Christopher Oram
Lighting Designer   Paule Constable
Music and Sound Score Composer   Adam Cork

The production transferred with the same cast to the Gielgud Theatre, London, on 28 January 2005, presented by Matthew Byam Shaw, Act Productions and Matthew Mitchell.

The text that follows is adapted from Schiller's original play. During the course of the rehearsal period, changes were made by the adapter, director and actors in order to accommodate the style of the production. The three most significant of these are indicated in this edition of the text.

DON CARLOS

For Derek, Richard, Claire, Elliot,
Charlotte, Una, Ian, Michael, Paul,
Roger, Brian, Andrew, Stuart and Peter

Characters

KING PHILIP II *of Spain and the Netherlands*

DON CARLOS, *the Crown Prince, his son*

QUEEN ELIZABETH, *daughter of Henry II of France*

RODRIGO, *Marquis of Posa, a Knight of Malta, Carlos' friend*

PRINCESS EBOLI, *a lady-in-waiting*

DUCHESS OF OLIVAREZ, *chief lady-in-waiting*

DUKE OF ALBA, *the King's adviser and military commander*

DOMINGO, *the King's confessor*

ALEXANDER FARNESE, PRINCE OF PARMA,
   the King's eighteen-year-old nephew

COUNT LERMA, *the King's chamberlain*

DUKE OF MEDINA SIDONIA, *Admiral of the Fleet,
   commander of the Spanish Armada*

COUNT CORDUA, *Head of Security*

GABRIEL DE LA CUEVA, *a page to the Queen*

THE CARDINAL GRAND INQUISITOR

LORDS, LADIES, PAGES, SOLDIERS,
   DOMINICAN MONKS, SERVANTS *and* GUARDS

ACT ONE

Scene One

*Sunshine through the window. Heat. But the room is in near
darkness.* DOMINGO, *kneeling. He has been kneeling for
a long time.* CARLOS *looks as if he's falling apart mentally
and physically.* DOMINGO *begins hesitantly.*

DOMINGO.
  Royal Highness . . .

  The Court, the Church, all Spain had hoped
  these pleasant days of rest in Aranjuez
  would restore your spirits . . .

  But there's been no progress . . .
  None – none at all . . .
  Forgive me.

  Royal Highness.

  CARLOS *motions him to stand.*

  Would you hide for ever from the sun?
  Will you not – at the very least –
  see your father – confide in him?
  Open your heart to him?
  Sir, your melancholy unsettles His Imperial Majesty –
  it distresses us all.
  I rack this weak brain of mine,
  yet can think of no blessing
  the Heavens have not abundantly bestowed upon you.
  The Old World and the New lie at your feet –
  What's left to sigh for?
  What could a son ask, a father would not grant?
  What would so great an Emperor as is your father
  refuse his Empire's heir?

  If only you'd be reconciled.

Why shut yourself away?
Step back into the sunlight, Prince.
In here there's only darkness – silence –
Eight months!
Eight wearisome months all Spain has wept for you –
Her troubled King lies waking,
Her Queen, your mother, finds no rest –

CARLOS.
The Queen –

DOMINGO.
Your mother, Prince.

CARLOS.
My true mother lost her life giving me life . . .
This new mother kills the love between a father and his son –
or what in him once passed for love –

DOMINGO.
You cannot blame the Queen for your estrangement!
No – I cannot think it! Could you hate her, Prince –
whom all Spain loves?

Open, open your heart to me!
You're in need of counsel, friendship – and confession.

CARLOS.
I confess I need a friend.

DOMINGO.
Then trust me, Prince. I labour only for your good.

CARLOS.
Truly?

DOMINGO.
I swear by Holy Church.

CARLOS.
Your secret's safe.
I'll not reveal it to my father.

DOMINGO (*alarmed*).
Reveal?

CARLOS.

> If King Philip learns you divide
> loyalty with his disloyal son
> It's goodbye to your cardinal's hat.

DOMINGO.

> The offices of Holy Church are not mocked –

CARLOS.

> God forbid!

DOMINGO.

> Don Carlos,
> As a man, your well-wisher, I will not pry
> and probe the secret of your sorrow . . .
> As your priest I must say this
> There is a sanctuary for world-weary souls
> safe haven for a raw and wounded conscience:
> our Holy Church, I mean – first mother to us all.
> She keeps our crimes, committed or intended,
> sealed up, secure, and locked away.
> My secrecy's a sacrament.
> I need say no more.

CARLOS.

> Yet . . . you would be tempted.

DOMINGO.

> You don't trust me?

CARLOS.

> The world speaks of you as a holy man.
> But – speaking plainly –
> it's my father's world that speaks of your holiness.
> You're the King's confessor –
> His Majesty tempts you with scarlet robes.
> So . . .
> Devote your service to the King alone –
> Keep loyalty undivided.
> Not all roads lead to Rome.

DOMINGO.

> Royal Highness –

CARLOS.
You've leave to go.

DOMINGO.
Today the King will return to the Capital.
The Court –

CARLOS.
You have leave. I'll follow to Madrid.

DOMINGO.
Royal Highness.

*Low bow. As he is about to exit backwards, the door opens
and a SERVANT announces:*

SERVANT
The Marquis of Posa.

CARLOS, *amazed, stands and turns his back on them both.*
RODRIGO *kneels to* CARLOS. DOMINGO *exits
backwards.* SERVANT *closes the door.* CARLOS *turns, lifts
up* RODRIGO *and embraces him.*

CARLOS.
Now God be thanked! Rodrigo!

He falls into RODRIGO's *arms.*

RODRIGO.
Prince –

CARLOS.
Oh how this strong embrace revives my fainting heart –

RODRIGO.
Carlos –

CARLOS.
I prayed for strength – a comforter –
God sends an angel from the Courts of Heaven –

RODRIGO.
What's this! –

CARLOS.
My friend – my only friend –

RODRIGO.

Calm, calm yourself –

CARLOS.

You've been away so long –

RODRIGO.

I've been in Flanders.

CARLOS.

In Flanders.

Looks into RODRIGO's *eyes. He begins to sink back into gloom.*

RODRIGO.

You're trembling –
such weakness – such a change – your looks, your bearing –
Are you ill?
Won't you speak to me, Carlos?

CARLOS.

You'd speak of Flanders. (*Breaking the embrace.*)

RODRIGO.

We must, we must . . .
I come to you –

CARLOS.

No – Rodrigo –

RODRIGO.

A true friend to a friendless land – they're your people,
Carlos . . .
In my sorrow, Flanders weeps upon your neck –
With my voice, she cries to you –

CARLOS.

You've come for Flanders, not for me.

RODRIGO.

I've come for you – Carlos – *for* Flanders.
They're saying – it's rumoured everywhere
your father will appoint, a viceroy in the Netherlands –
The Duke of Alba –

CARLOS.
More dog than duke –

RODRIGO.
Alba! – enemy to change, the torment of our times,
old scourge of new thinking –
If Alba's sent to chain our freedom-loving people
in the rusty manacles of Spanish law –
if this dog once gets Flanders by the throat –
All life will be worried from her –
the flame of her new faith will gutter and snuff out.

Carlos,
It's time to act.
Great Charles the Fifth, your grandfather,
loved this land. In you, heir to his greatness,
the people have placed their hopes.
Flanders will fall if you desert her cause.

CARLOS.
Then let her fall.

RODRIGO.
Answer like yourself – Carlos!

CARLOS.
I'm not Carlos!
I've awakened from a dream. Nothing more.
There was a time – a dream of freedom –
Freedom! – the word alone could fire my blood –
'When I am King of Spain!' – Remember? –
We'd talk of bringing in a Golden Age –
awakening a world of childish hopes. (*Through tears.*)

RODRIGO.
Dreams, Prince – only dreams?

CARLOS (*collapsing in* RODRIGO*'s arms*).
Say nothing – let me weep a world of tears –
my heart – my heart! – lost in the vastness
of a father's power –
I've no one – no single soul in all this world . . .
Everywhere, everything, and everyone is his!
My father's Empire outruns imagination –

Wherever winds blow, ships bear Spain's bloody banners –
There's nowhere – no place upon this earth
I may set down the burden of my grief –
only here – here upon your breast.

By all that was ever holy to us, Rodrigo,
by all our hopes and dreams,
Do not dislodge me from this sanctuary.

RODRIGO.
Dearer to me than all the world –

CARLOS.
Childhood. Happiness.
How I tormented you with affection! –
Offering my heart
and receiving in return
only the duty, coldness, and courtesy
the Court of Spain demands.
Form! Ritual! Ceremony!
What comes from nature – from here – (*Striking his heart.*)
must be clenched in, suppressed, concealed, denied –

I wanted your love.
I wanted one living, human soul
To call me Carlos . . . not 'Royal Highness' –
Your love –

RODRIGO.
I gave it –

CARLOS.
You remember?

RODRIGO.
I do – But, Carlos –

CARLOS.
Remember a group of boys playing a game of tennis? –
The Queen of Bohemia – my aunt – who came to watch –
hit in the face, by a ball you struck? –
and we – being boys – we laughed.

The King my father –
My father –

Who never was a child,
nor ever played any game –
nor ever, I think, once smiled –
saw only the insult to the Queen,
and chose to believe the affront deliberate.
O those terrifying rages! –
He swore he'd find and flog the guilty boy.
Rodrigo, I saw you tremble – turn pale . . .
'Father,' I cried, 'punish me.
I struck my Aunt, I hurt the Queen!'
I took your flogging –

RODRIGO.
I remember –

CARLOS.
As his fists struck me down,
I saw you weep.
I'd won your heart –

RODRIGO.
You keep it still –

CARLOS.
I need it – now more than ever.
Hear my confession
then teach me how I may find absolution –

RODRIGO.
Carlos –

CARLOS.
Shh – Say nothing – nothing.
I love Elizabeth – my father's wife.

RODRIGO *is dumbstruck.*

Now speak if you can –
Tell me no wretch beneath the Heavens
suffers as I do – say it!

RODRIGO.
I came for a lion in defence of Flanders' cause –
I find a lovesick boy.

CARLOS.
In every expression of contempt I'm there before you –

RODRIGO.
Carlos –

CARLOS.
No – you'll find no word of comfort.
The world, the Court, human nature, Rome! –
all combine – conspire in my destruction –
My father's wife! –

My destiny, at worst, is madness –
at best incarceration – death –
Even to look at her – Spain's Empress –
is a kind of treason!
And still my love grows!

RODRIGO.
Does she know?

CARLOS.
Think! You're back in Spain!
Rigid ceremony – the antique ritual of the court –
There are walls of brass between me and the Queen.
How can I ever speak to her alone?
My father's spies are everywhere –
Is this a father!
I was six years old before I was taken to him – a child, an
innocent –
'What are you doing, sir,' I asked.
'Signing death warrants.'
Imagine! – his face . . . expressionless.
No recognition of me as his son –
No smile, no love – nothing – a blank.
And so we have continued. Blank.
Unless I was sent for punishment –
Then anger, disappointment and contempt –
Dear God! Let's not speak of my father –
And yet . . .
I had one precious thing I thought my own:
Elizabeth . . .
betrothed to me with oaths as strong as marriage vows.

Two mighty nations – the Valois' France, my father's Spain
combined to seal and bless the match –
The Church and Heaven made us swear our love –
I swore. I loved . . .
I kept my vows – I keep them still.
My father married her.

O the torment! – to see her every day –
forced to hide my love
behind arthritic gestures of form and courtesy –
while my youth – my passion is inwardly blazing.
O my true friend, to be alone with her –
to tell her I love her still –
what would I not give?
My life for a single moment!

RODRIGO.
She's your father's wife.
That's an end of it.

CARLOS.
Of all the fathers in the world
why do the Heavens punish me with him?
Of all sons that could have pleased a king
why was God pleased
to displease this King with me?
No two minds are more at odds,
yet here we remain – we three – unnaturally linked
in a single chain of love. Impossible equation!
Wretched, wretched fate!

RODRIGO.
Listen to me, Carlos –
Be guided by me –

CARLOS.
I will.
Whatever our love demands
I will perform.

RODRIGO.
First, I'll seek an audience with the Queen.
I've letters for her out of France –

If she's that same Elizabeth I befriended
at her father's Court, she will receive me.
I doubt that stifling Spanish politesse
has smothered up a French girl's joie de vivre.
If any love for Carlos lingers in her heart
I'll find it out.

CARLOS.
Only to speak to her –
To speak to her . . . Elizabeth.

Scene Two

Heat. The QUEEN's private garden at Aranjuez. PRINCESS EBOLI stands looking bored – hints that she is slightly unstable. The DUCHESS OF OLIVAREZ (Olee'bareth), stands, alert and on guard, QUEEN ELIZABETH is seated. All have fans which they use all the time – either to fan themselves or to hide their faces.

ELIZABETH.
You are impatient to return to Madrid, Princess Eboli.

EBOLI.
Madame, I confess, I am.

ELIZABETH.
Do you dislike the countryside so much?

EBOLI.
Madame, I love the Capital.

ELIZABETH.
What's loveable there? To me, Madrid's a graveyard.
Your opinion, Duchess Olivarez?

OLIVAREZ.
Madame, I have no opinion.
It is the custom of the Court
to spend this month in Aranjuez,

another at the Imperial Hunting Lodge,
and to pass the winter in the Winter Palace.
This has been the custom
Since custom first gave Spain her kings.
We should fear change.
What seems a forward step may prove a backward one.

OLIVAREZ *curtseys.*

ELIZABETH.
My heart aches! – to bid farewell to all this beauty . . .
I love the wildness God has lent us here.
Beyond these walls Nature is free – innocent as childhood –
the flowers – the birds and little jewelled insects
come and go as they please without form and ceremony . . .
Sometimes, imagining their freedom, I am free myself –
as if caressed by the gentle breeze
of my beloved France.

Do you frown?
My homeland holds me still –
Childhood memories reign in my heart –
but I will not forget that I am Queen of Spain.

OLIVAREZ.
Madame, there will be bullfights in Madrid
and a great Auto da Fe –

ELIZABETH.
Killing and burning –

OLIVAREZ *registers confusion.*

EBOLI.
Those to be burned, Madame, are heretics –

OLIVAREZ.
The body is burned but the soul is saved.

ELIZABETH.
Let's think of joyful things – where's my child?

OLIVAREZ.
Madame, it's not yet time.

ELIZABETH.
  I wish to see my little girl.

OLIVAREZ.
  It's not the customary hour –

ELIZABETH.
  I wish . . .

  She stands up impatiently. They all kneel. She resigns herself.

  I wish . . .

  Be good enough to inform me, Duchess Olivarez,
  When it's time for me to be a mother.

  She sits down again. They all stand. Enter PAGE.

  I had such hopes of my time here in Aranjuez,
  Do all hopes come to nothing?

PAGE (*bowing to* OLIVAREZ).
  Your Grace – (*He whispers to her.*)

ELIZABETH.
  Time's without motion here – each new day a shadow of
  every other –
  Nothing's moving at all.
  I'm beginning to forget
  what my hopes once were. (*Shudders.*)

OLIVAREZ.
  Madame, Your Majesty, a problem of etiquette presents
  itself –
  The Marquis of Posa is in attendance.

ELIZABETH.
  Posa?

OLIVAREZ.
  He has been in Flanders, and in France –

ELIZABETH.
  Then he's been in Paradise –

OLIVAREZ.

And begs leave to kiss your hand.
He brings letters from your mother.

ELIZABETH.

And the problem?

OLIVAREZ.

I can think of no precedent, Madame – none at all.
He's a nobleman of Castile – and also a knight of Malta.
He begs leave to deliver letters from your mother, who is also a queen,
a foreign power, and Regent of France –

ELIZABETH.

Am I not permitted to receive my mother's letters?

OLIVAREZ.

Well, yes . . . That's the problem . . . I'm unsure . . .
Nor are we in Your Majesty's audience chamber.
Here in the open air –

ELIZABETH.

We will receive the Marquis.

OLIVAREZ.

But –

ELIZABETH.

If custom is offended, let the offence be mine.

OLIVAREZ.

Then I must beg Your Majesty's permission to withdraw –
I cannot be seen to countenance –

ELIZABETH.

The Duchess best knows what duty requires of her.
You have our leave to go.

The PAGE *goes to fetch* RODRIGO.

EBOLI.

Marquis Posa – is he not a friend of the Crown Prince,
Madame?

ELIZABETH.
Of Don Carlos? Why do you ask?

Looks searchingly at EBOLI *who blushes.*

Ah, Eboli, are you in love?
You're blushing –

EBOLI *veils and takes up a position standing in front of*
ELIZABETH *who holds her fan in front of her face.*

PAGE.
The Marquis Posa.

RODRIGO *enters and kneels.*

ELIZABETH.
Welcome home, Marquis.
The Queen of Spain welcomes you from her dearest France.
Princess – (*She curtseys.*)
This brave gentleman bore my favour on his helm
in the great tournament at Rheims,
and broke lances with the late King, my father.

They cross themselves.

By this Marquis I was first tempted into the sin of Pride.
To be Queen of so proud a nation of flatterers,
I thought, must be something.

RODRIGO.
In those days, Your Majesty, I little thought the King of
France
would so easily grant us the only French possession
Spain had a mind to take.

ELIZABETH.
A flatterer still? – And a daring one.
I think Spain has a mind to take the world.

RODRIGO.
And I dare think – dare *say* – such things
only now you are Spain's Queen.

ELIZABETH.
The letters from my mother?

RODRIGO (*handing them over*).
   I found her in low spirits, Madame –
   The government of France is a heavy a burden
   for one to bear alone. Her consolation
   is the pleasure she takes in her daughter's happiness –
   being Queen of Spain.

ELIZABETH.
   Ah . . . Could a queen of Spain be less than happy?
   You're a traveller, M'sieur –
   You visit the courts of princes –
   study manners and philosophy –
   such freedom is to be envied – even of kings.
   Free men – free souls – free minds . . .
   You seek the cut and thrust of wit –
   Innovation – in the arts, the sciences –
   pleasure, society, laughter . . .
   To speak plainly, M'sieur –
   I doubt you'll find such things
   in Madrid.

RODRIGO.
   Madrid, at least,
   is spared the horrors of war, Madame.
   Flanders is less fortunate.

ELIZABETH.
   You've come from Flanders?
   I grieve for her people –

EBOLI (*warning*).
   Madame –

ELIZABETH.
   They shield me from all talk of bloodshed.
   Eboli, those flowers over there – the blue ones –
   what are they?

EBOLI.
   Madame, they are hyacinths.

ELIZABETH.
   Hyacinths? At this time of year – nonsense!
   Fetch me some of them.

EBOLI *goes.*

Unless I am much mistaken
your return has brought happiness
to one other soul.

RODRIGO.
Madame – I fear not so.
One alone can make that person happy –
We both know it's not in my power –

ELIZABETH (*speaking urgently and low*).
Rodrigo –
Tell Carlos – I command him as his Queen –
implore him by the innocent love between us –
he must abandon all thoughts of me,
shake off his childish infatuation, and become a man!
He shames himself! Does he think I do not see? –

Destiny will raise Carlos above us all –
place sceptres in his hand – crowns upon his head –
give millions of souls into his keeping.

Say this to the Prince:
He cannot – must not – abandon his people
for faded dreams of what we might have been.
That's finished – done with – childishness.

One day soon he'll be King – what may he not do then?
With his father's diadem upon his head, the holy oil upon
his brow, he may revoke his father's edicts –
dismiss his father's ministers, end his wars, topple down his
monuments – Who dare stop him?
But one thing he can never do – never, *never* do –
He cannot take his father's wife.
He cannot make me his Queen.

EBOLI *returns with flowers.*

And now it must be time –
Princess, fetch my daughter to me.

She backs out.

I was Carlos' first love

but Heaven overruled his hopes . . . and mine.
Let him accept it.
Endure it
as I do.

*ELIZABETH beckons RODRIGO aside and slips him a
letter she has concealed in her Bible.*

Now he must love his people as he once loved me –
be their prince – their champion. Theirs is the worthier cause.
I wrote this for his sake.

RODRIGO.
Do you love him still?
Will you see him – speak to him?

*Suddenly enter OLIVAREZ looking horrified, COUNT
LERMA, the DUKE OF ALBA – then KING PHILIP,
COUNT CORDUA – and any others but not the DUKE
OF MEDINA SIDONIA, nor the PRINCE OF PARMA.
ELIZABETH curtseys, RODRIGO kneels. PHILIP,
displeased, takes in the scene.*

PHILIP.
Alone, Madame? Alone?

ELIZABETH.
Majesty –

PHILIP.
Alone.
Which ladies are in attendance today?
Whose office is it to wait upon the Queen?

ELIZABETH.
Husband –
The fault is mine.
I asked the Princess Eboli –

PHILIP.
Eboli –

ELIZABETH.
To fetch our daughter.

PHILIP.

> You send the Princess Eboli
> to do the office of a chambermaid?
>
> There's reproach in her looks.
> My wife judges me harsh when, out of love,
> I'm careful of her honour.
>
> God and the gentlemen of my Court
> bear witness when I swear
> these eyes will never droop in sleep at each day's end
> until I have remembered in my prayers, the vastness of my
> lands, and the mumbled hopes and fears
> of my meanest subject.
> But I tell you, Madame – God searches my heart –
> there, He sees, my care of you
> raised high above the needs of empire.
> Is this not a marriage?
> What are crowns, what are kingdoms? Dust and ashes –
> Duke Alba's sword ensures my people keep the faith.
> But a wife's love? – her loyalty?
> Well . . . God gives husbands eyes.

ELIZABETH.

> And when your wife gives cause for doubt –

PHILIP.

> They tell me I'm the foremost man in Christendom –
> upon my lands the sun for ever shines.
> I possess riches beyond the reach of thought
> but what's possession?
> The world was once my father's – today it's mine –
> tomorrow Destiny will give it to my son.
> But this – this – is mine. This is possession.

> *Takes* ELIZABETH's *hand.*

> God's given me kingdoms –
> The King has taken Elizabeth for himself.
> And only Death can filch her from me.

ELIZABETH.

> We are all mortal.

PHILIP.
These grey hairs say as much.

ELIZABETH.
Do you fear?

PHILIP.
Whenever, wherever I encounter fear (*Searching her face.*)
my instinct is to strike at it.

Where is Don Carlos? Who's seen the Prince?

No response.

First in rank, last to show duty – He avoids me.
It hasn't gone unnoticed.
Hot blood, cold looks, solitary –
something unhealthy broods beneath his melancholy.
Do we sense danger there?
My son, my Empire's heir – the hope of Spain,
he must not go unwatched –
Alba.

ALBA.
Majesty –

PHILIP.
You are my sword and shield.
Is my son a danger to me?

ALBA.
Majesty, he will not go unwatched.

Puts his hand on his sword.

LERMA.
Majesty, duty requires me to set aside humility
and contradict the wisest king in Christendom:
I may never believe so noble a father
could breed unworthy sons.
The Prince has a wildness of spirit
but his heart's your own.

PHILIP (*a moment's anger, then a searching look*).
A father thanks you for those comfortable words,
Count Lerma.

The King, however, places his trust in Alba's sword.
No more.
You, sir –

RODRIGO kneels and kisses his hand.

Follow us to Madrid.

Exit RODRIGO.

The abomination of heresy fevers my people –
Murmuring Flanders seethes in revolt –
Now comes Judgement Day.
Destiny has made me God's Regent on Earth –
custodian of conscience – scourge of heretics.
Pray for me, lords, as with blood and fire
I lop away the rotting limb
and fight to restore the purity of the True Faith.
I have many souls to save,
and the instrument God places in my hands – is terror . . .
Terror.
Tomorrow, when the bonfires of Grace blaze in Madrid –
let all Europe bear witness –
Spain is growing too hot for heresy.

Come, Madame.

He bows to ELIZABETH. She curtseys.

Exeunt PHILIP with QUEEN ELIZABETH followed by the others, strictly according to rank.

Scene Three

*CARLOS, followed by RODRIGO, enters with the letter.
He is purposeful, different in appearance, and quite unlike
the CARLOS of the first scene.*

CARLOS.
Resolved.
Everything she demands, I'll perform.
Because she wishes it, I'll dedicate myself to Flanders.

RODRIGO.

> We've little time.
> The King's Council has named Alba Viceroy.

CARLOS.

> But the King has not yet approved the nomination –
> the instruments are not yet signed and sealed –
> nor will they be if I can prevent it.
> Listen, Rodrigo –
> I've never asked him anything –
> Now I'll beg an apprenticeship
> and learn the craft of kingship –
> The Crown Prince begs employment of the Crown –
> No! – I'll not beg – I'll demand! –
> What do you think – how can he deny me, Rodrigo?
> He's wise – he'll see the justice of it.

> I have a deeper purpose:
> I hope, with the boldness of this action, to make him proud.
> I want the King to see an image of his youthful self in me –
> and – loving what he sees – applaud the Prince
> but smile upon the son.

RODRIGO.

> How could he refuse?
> This is the Carlos I thought was lost.

CARLOS.

> You found him when he could not find himself –
> leaving him for ever in your debt.

RODRIGO.

> For ever?

CARLOS.

> For ever.
> Here – embrace me.

> If ever flattery would steal my heart –
> When from these eyes no tears of pity flow
> When my ears are stopped to mercy –
> stand firm and be the guardian of my soul.
> Lay open all my faults and failures,
> fears and weaknesses –

And when the day comes for me to take the throne
hold fast the King as you do now the Prince –
speak harsh truths in friendship's voice.
Together – we've nothing to fear.

RODRIGO.
Best make a friend of fear – for our cause is dangerous . . .
I am dangerous to kings.
How can the Crown of Spain embrace a Flanders heretic?
Carlos, we must conceal our friendship.
Before the Court we must be Prince and subject.

He kneels and kisses CARLOS' *hand.*

ACT TWO

Scene Four

KING PHILIP*'s private chapel.* DOMINGO *gives* PHILIP,
who is kneeling at the altar rail, communion. ALBA,
impatient, waiting to receive his commission, stands in armour.
Other LORDS *and* SECRETARIES *wait.* PHILIP *comes out of*
the chapel. A SECRETARY *hands him the commission. As he*
does so, CARLOS *enters and approaches* PHILIP. *Without*
thinking, ALBA *takes a single step forward, intercepting him.*

CARLOS.
The Crown Prince takes precedence over a duke.

ALBA *hesitates – everybody else withdraws quickly.*

But I will give place before a Minister of State.
The Duke of Alba speaks for Spain –
mine's merely a family matter.

He smiles at ALBA, *bows and steps back.*

PHILIP.
The Duke will stand aside if the Crown Prince
wishes to speak.

ALBA *takes one step back.*

CARLOS.
Then, oblige me, Duke of Alba:
You wouldn't wish to hear the trifling confidences
between a father and his child.

PHILIP.
He'll listen to what you have to say.
The Duke is Spain's friend.

CARLOS.
Mine too, I hope.

PHILIP.

> Flattery?
> When have you earned Alba's friendship or desired it?

CARLOS.

> Majesty – we must not dishonour the Duke –
> let's not have him play the eavesdropper –

PHILIP (*with an angry look at* CARLOS).

> Alba, withdraw.

> ALBA *bows and goes into an inner chamber behind the arras.*

CARLOS.

> Father, give me your hand –
> then ask a blessing on this day! – too long, too long
> I have been absent from your heart –

> *Great emotion. He kneels, kisses* PHILIP's *hand and clings onto it.*

PHILIP (*under his breath, embarrassed*).

> Get up –

CARLOS.

> Father – what have I done? How have I offended you? –

PHILIP.

> Spare us the playhouse pathos –

CARLOS.

> I am sincere –
> Look into my eyes – read artlessness there.
> Or am I victim of some courtiers' malice? –
> your murmuring lords, your whispering priests –

PHILIP.

> Can I believe your heart is pure?
> That in your prayers you remember me?

CARLOS.

> We must be reconciled –
> Now – seize this moment – lay ceremony aside –
> Speak as my father and I'll answer like your son.
> Make peace between us. Let's swear our love

and angels – Heaven itself – will pour down blessings
upon our holy act.
Let me steal back into your heart – (*Clasps* PHILIP'*s knees.*)

PHILIP.
Don't touch me! Take your hands away – Get up!

CARLOS.
Father –

PHILIP.
I despise such shows –

CARLOS.
Shows! A son's love? –

PHILIP.
I blush to see it on display!

CARLOS' *eyes fill with tears.*

O now the tears! Are you a man?
Humiliate yourself if you must –
but not in my presence –
Out! Out!

CARLOS.
Take me back!

PHILIP.
Get out of my sight!

Come to me from the field of battle – in glory or disgrace –
victory or defeat – I'll open wide these arms to take you back.
But not like this – this is shaming – I blush for you.
Shaming! Tears? – I have a milksop for a son.
When have you ever tried to be a man?

CARLOS.
Tears show humanity.
Have you never wept?
Oh Father, learn a little of this art
or one day you may shed a lifetime's tears
and not know how to stop the flow –

PHILIP.
Words! Soft words! – They won't soften my distrust –

CARLOS.
Distrust?
Who's made you doubt me?
Alba? Domingo, your confessor?
Who are my slanderers?

PHILIP.
Good men!
Spain's ministers – their loyalty's proven –
tested, tried, found true.
You'll show them more respect.

CARLOS.
I will not.
I'll pay respect where it's due –

PHILIP.
What arrogance!

CARLOS.
Am I not more to you than Alba –
a mercenary – a hired sword?
What I'll do, I do for love – of you and of our land.
Why should Alba care that you stagger
under the weight of a crown he'll never wear? –
You're not Alba's father!
Why should he weep to watch you growing old –
Feared and unloved – for ever alone –
Alone.

PHILIP *is thrown by the word.*

Deprived of a son who'd love you –
no comfort in your loneliness but power – possession –
Who would not weep for you?

PHILIP (*not unmoved*).
I am alone.

CARLOS.
No longer.
Don't hate me.
I'll love you like a child.
Don't hate me.

I've so much love to give you.
Only don't hate me.

Is there a father who takes no delight in memories
of the son he loved in childhood –
the man's stride slowing to tiny steps –
pausing – smiling – hand in hand
down the sweet lanes of remembrance –
dreaming a glorious future for them both?
And then the father living in the son's achievement
reaping golden harvests from the seeds of his love?

Or were you never so?
Did the childless holy men who rule your life
exclude you from a paradise, forbidden to them?

PHILIP (*not unmoved*).
O my son, my son!
You betray yourself – fine words but empty ones.
When were you ever such a son to me?

CARLOS.
May God forgive you.
He sees how you shut me out! –
Out of government – and out of your affection.
You exclude me from office in a land I'll one day rule!
You are to blame – unjust – unfatherly –
Can't you see the shame you put upon me?

PHILIP.
You're not yet fit for office!
You're impulsive – all heart, no head.
You'd tear down everything I've built –

CARLOS.
Some things should be torn down – bad things destroyed –
so that the good and new may be raised up.
I'll no longer live in idleness –
I've come with a request.

PHILIP.
A request? Name it.

CARLOS.

The army of Flanders.

PHILIP.

No! It needs a man to command it. Not a boy. No.

CARLOS.

But I'm loved in Flanders.

The grandson of Charles the Fifth will accomplish more with love

Than Alba could with terror, fire and sword –

PHILIP.

No. You're a dreamer.

CARLOS.

True! And I'm human, Father! –

Nobody – not even you – would claim that for the Duke of Alba.

PHILIP.

My son . . . (*Patiently.*) Flanders totters on the edge of bloody rebellion –

if I show mercy now, it will be perceived as weakness.

Terror's the answer. And Alba was born to terrorise.

On the field of battle a soft-hearted commander's less use than a coward.

You're not a soldier – don't ask this of me –

CARLOS.

How could you know what mercy might achieve?

When have you ever shown pity? – in anything?

Just once, I beg you, place your trust in me.

What have you to lose?

When Flanders hears I am coming –

The Prince of Spain! – banners flying! –

there will be no rebellion.

I'll bring them hope –

freedom – fair dealing – the rule of law.

But Alba? All Alba would do is lay waste our good lands.

'He'd make a desert and call it peace.'

Show some faith in me – trust me with Flanders.

PHILIP (*studying* CARLOS*' face intently*).
    And let you risk my finest army among rebels?
    Place a sword at my own throat?

CARLOS.
    That was unworthy.

After a pause, subdued and urgent.

    Can you sit unmoved by everything I've said?
    Will you brush me aside –
    dismiss me – leave my mind in such turmoil?
    Father – for the sake of my reason
    I need some sign – some show of trust from you.
    Can't you understand?
    Think how you'll dishonour me –
    if you refuse me everything – everything – everything –
    What will the world say of me?
    Am I unfit to be your successor?

    O Father –
    Let me make one last appeal:

He begins to lose control.

    Don't place your throne in the hands of Churchmen –
    Don't let Alba usurp my place –
    Don't leave me weeping at your feet.
    Will you humiliate me in front of the Court?
    Give me something – something to hope for.
    Show the world I'm your son.
    Let me govern Flanders.

PHILIP.
    You've had my answer.
    Pursue this further and you risk my anger.

CARLOS.
    Grant me this favour.
    Honour me with this commission!

PHILIP (*with forced self-control*).
    No.
    My son, you seem unwell.

And – if that's the case – how could I part with you?
You're in need of help, my own physicians . . .

CARLOS *gives a look of contempt for the subterfuge.*

The Duke goes to Flanders – it's for the best.

CARLOS (*distracted*).
Hover above me, angels and powers –

PHILIP.
Stop that, Carlos!
Are you quite unmanned? –

CARLOS.
So this is how it must be between us?
Nothing changes?

No answer.

The Duke of Alba rather than your own son?
Your word is final?

PHILIP.
It's the word of a king.

CARLOS.
It's the word of my father.

CARLOS *exits in high emotion.* PHILIP *reflects gloomily
for some moments, then paces up and down as if trying to
decide something.*

PHILIP.
Alba!

ALBA *comes guiltily from where he has been listening.*
PHILIP *takes up* ALBA's *papers.*

The instruments. Signed and sealed.
You're ready to march?

ALBA.
Yes, Majesty. I have been ready for some time.

PHILIP (*looks searchingly at him*).
Have you?
Go take your leave of the Queen.

And the Crown Prince . . .
Part from him kindly – offer him humble service
and all duty.

ALBA.

Your Majesty seems troubled.
The Prince departed in some anger –
Perhaps you spoke of –

PHILIP.

You. Yes – you were our theme, Alba.
It means nothing to me – nothing –
that His Royal Highness hates my advisers . . .
But to be told *why* he despises them
has given me pause for thought.

ALBA *turns pale and is about to reply.*

No – I'm not interested in excuses – understand me:
Make your peace with the Prince
before your armies leave for Flanders.

ALBA (*low bow*).

Majesty.

PHILIP.

One thing more, sir. Remind me –

Looking hard at ALBA.

Who poisoned my mind against my son?
I listened only to you.
Why have I never given him a fair hearing?
From this day I'll keep the Prince much closer to the throne.
Leave us.

ALBA *leaves in some confusion.*

Scene Five

A corridor near QUEEN ELIZABETH'*s apartments.*
CARLOS, *still distracted, is intercepted by the* PAGE *who gives him a letter and a key.*

CARLOS.
No, wait, boy. Who sent this key? This letter?

PAGE.
A lady, Royal Highness.

CARLOS.
What lady! – Dear God! – can it be? –
(*To himself.*) O my heart, my heart!

PAGE.
I can't reveal her name, sir. I'm sworn to secrecy –
But she wishes you to come to her at once.
The letter directs you to a locked room
in the Queen's apartments –

CARLOS.
Keep your voice down! –

PAGE.
A safe place where you may speak freely.
You'll not be overheard.

CARLOS.
What are you?

PAGE.
A page in the household of Her Majesty.
A son of the old nobility –

CARLOS.
Is this some trap? Did the King send you?
Domingo, his confessor? – whose hand's in this? –
Come, come! If you value your life – tell me the truth.

PAGE.
I'm no liar, sir. I swear
on the honour of my family.

CARLOS *seems to accept this.*

CARLOS.
Now listen – listen carefully.
Think that the light of day, the air you breathe,
your most trusted friends, are the King's spies.
This letter you've brought's a powder keg;
If you remember it tomorrow – repeat what you've done or
said –
to anyone – a lord, a Churchman, the King himself –
all of us are dead men – we'll be blown to fragments.

PAGE.
Sir, you terrify me –

CARLOS.
I mean to.
Pray you'll never know what terrors you've unleashed –

Enter ALBA.

Go, now – Quickly –
we've not spoken – you've given me nothing –

PAGE.
Royal Highness. (*Bows low and exits in a hurry.*)

ALBA.
Royal Highness. A word with you. (*Bows low.*)

CARLOS.
If you wish. Some other time, though.

CARLOS *ignores him. Exeunt in different directions.*

Scene Six

The PRINCESS EBOLI's *apartment. A veiled figure sitting.*
CARLOS *enters.*

CARLOS (*almost inaudible*).
Madame.

He kneels. She unveils.

EBOLI.
Royal Highness.

CARLOS, *recognising her, is covered in confusion.*

CARLOS.
Princess Eboli . . . Where am I?
I must have mistaken – (*Bows, about to leave.*)

EBOLI (*attempting to appear light-hearted*).
You are welcome, sir – Don't go –

CARLOS.
Lady, I cannot –

EBOLI.
The chamber's secure –

He sinks down.

We'll not be overheard.
Say something. Say anything.

CARLOS.
Are these not the Queen's apartments?

EBOLI.
Set your mind at rest – she won't suspect –
A soul so pure as hers imagines nothing less in others.
She's innocent of this intrigue.

CARLOS *puts his head in his hands.*

Oh, sir! –
I beg you – throw off melancholy. (*She attempts a lightness.*)
If you could know how long I've pitied you!
You seem near to despair –

CARLOS.
I could despair –

EBOLI.
Prince?
Carlos – will you not then – for want of a better friend –
confide in me?
Am I unworthy of such honour?

CARLOS.
  I know you mean well –

EBOLI.
  Then what can I do? –

CARLOS.
  Nothing –

EBOLI.
  But –

CARLOS.
  Unless you'd speak to my father.
  It's said you have influence with the King. (*He turns away.*)

EBOLI (*under her breath, shock which she tries to hide*).
  Who says so!

CARLOS.
  I had a foolish dream.
  I had made up my mind to be gone from here.
  I wished to write myself into the book of fame
  by accomplishing a bloodless victory in Flanders.

EBOLI.
  I thought –
  the whole Court knows you've spoken to the King –
  Everybody is saying he'll give you Alba's armies.

CARLOS.
  My father doesn't say so . . .
  Princess.
  Why did you send me this key?

EBOLI (*becomes even more agitated, pacing up and down,
  trying to give herself the will to confess*).
  Oh Carlos – forgive me – I need your guidance –
  I'm helpless – in danger of disgrace –
  I have no friendly voice, no protector –

CARLOS (*astonished and sympathetic moves closer to her*).
  Dear lady – what can be the –

EBOLI.

Don't let them shame me! –

CARLOS.

Who –

EBOLI.

Don't let them make a whore of me –

CARLOS.

Make –

EBOLI.

Read the letter – it's in the letter –
I suspected nothing – I thought him a saint.

He glances at the letter, doesn't read it, hangs on her words.

God knows I've resisted –
But they wear me down, Carlos – they wear me down!
Without some virtuous friend – some steadying arm –
Heaven itself can't save me from a fall.
I am so weak – alone – very near madness, madness –

CARLOS.

Lady, I swear, you've nothing to fear –

EBOLI.

Love should be the reward of love –

CARLOS.

I won't fail you –

EBOLI.

I can't give myself where I am not loved.
The husband I choose I will worship for ever –
make him godlike in our happiness –
we'll find immortality together.
Don't let them force me! –
Did God create this poor body
for a lecher's pleasure? –

CARLOS.

Lady, lady –

EBOLI.

I should flee the Court –
spend a life in prayer – but I'm powerless –
I haven't the will – the courage to leave while . . .
My strength abandons me . . . the truth is . . .
I am desired – but not loved.
And where I am not loved – I love!

CARLOS.

You are, you are loved –
Don't be afraid.
I'll be your guardian – accept my protection.

EBOLI.

Carlos!
The way to your heart
is a winding, dangerous road
but at the end – how great will be her reward!

CARLOS.

Her reward?
Then you've guessed?

She takes his hand. He tries to withdraw it.

EBOLI.

I've known – how long I've known! – You are in love . . .
Carlos . . . Carlos – your love is returned.

CARLOS (*overjoyed*).

O –

EBOLI (*takes his hand*).

How pale – how beautiful! –
This hand holds an empire's most precious gifts:
Itself, to give away, and with the gift
a crown.

CARLOS.

I beg you – keep my secret safe.
I am in love –

EBOLI.

Is it so difficult – to speak her name?
Is it my part to say

I know –
I've always known you love me?

CARLOS.
. . . ?

EBOLI.
Protect me.

Dull realisation. A long silence.

O – madness! What have I said!

CARLOS.
Princess –

EBOLI.
Madness – Go! Go – for God's sake go!

CARLOS.
I can't abandon you in this distress –

EBOLI.
Madness – only madness – (*Laughs.*)
My shame! Oh the shame –
Don't look at me or I'll die of it –
Go – Leave me! Go!

He rushes to the door.

No! Give me back the letter –

CARLOS.
I've . . . What letter?

EBOLI.
The letter from the King! Give –

CARLOS (*looking at the letter and realising*).
From the King!

EBOLI.
Dear God! My God! He didn't know! You didn't –

CARLOS (*to himself*).
My father's her seducer!

EBOLI.
    Royal Highness –
    I'm in torment – the letter – the letter –

CARLOS.
    I'll keep it safe. (*Exit.*)

EBOLI.
    Elizabeth!
    They loved before his father married her –
    betrothed – changed rings – swore oaths upon the book.
    The Queen! – his father's wife!

    And she loves him . . .
    She does, she does – his lust's returned –
    passion could never endure so long unfed –
    They're lovers, sure – the boy and his mother –
    I see them! – naked – writhing in the royal sheets!
    Oh, what heat in his touch! –
    I felt her lips, her body burning in his embrace –
    What daring!

    And wretched King Philip's a cuckold –
    my would-be deceiver's deceived!

    Laughs.

    The King!

    Panic.

    Dear God! Carlos has my letter!
    How will he use it?
    What can he gain by his father's disgrace?

    But oh how skilfully she plays her game!
    We've all been hoodwinked – taken in –
    She's hot, she's hot – and the world thinks her a saint.
    Insatiable! – feeding at the father's royal table
    and banqueting at the son's.
    I worshipped her.
    And now they'll laugh at me.

    I'll laugh too, though . . . I'll laugh, I'll laugh . . .

Scene Seven

Hurrying past QUEEN ELIZABETH's *apartments,* CARLOS
*is studying the letter. He is exhilarated at the thought of the
hold he has over his father.* ALBA *enters from* ELIZABETH's
audience chamber having taken his leave.

ALBA.
Royal Highness, are you now at leisure?

CARLOS.
Be brief.

ALBA.
I owe you thanks, sir.

CARLOS.
Unlikely. For what?

ALBA.
I heard you pleading with the King,
and can only suppose it was on my behalf –
since His Majesty gave me my appointment
the moment you fled the presence.
Have you not heard? I am made Viceroy in Flanders.

CARLOS.
May God go with you, sir.
They'll have need of Him in Flanders.

ALBA.
Have you any commission for me?

CARLOS.
What possible commission could I have
for the Duke of Alba?

ALBA.
A proclamation for the Netherlands, perhaps?
There was talk in the Court of some urgent business you
had there.
It was even suggested you were hoping to lead my armies.

CARLOS.

I was – but now that's all forgotten.

It's in the past.

You and I must look to the future.

The King thinks you're the best General he has.

And so – for the present – you are.

I look to the future.

For now . . . Well . . .

ALBA.

What's it like, Prince, to lie on the soft bed of my victories –

dreaming of the crown you hope to wear?

Do you never give a thought to the suffering,

the deep wounds I've had, to feed those hopes and dreams?

This sword gave Spain her Empire –

it gave Spain's Empire the rule of law –

carved order out of chaos –

And shining before a bloody cross

it will slaughter the children of heresy.

God reigns in Heaven.

Leave me to be his judge on Earth.

CARLOS.

You've come too early, Duke.

ALBA.

What?

CARLOS.

In the Book of Revelation we may read –

'The Great Beast will lay waste the Earth

with famine, fire, sword, and bestial ferocity' –

But not until Judgement Day.

You're early.

ALBA.

Were you not a king's son –

CARLOS (*flaring up*).

What! What then –

ALBA.

I'd show you what your weapon's for, boy –

CARLOS (*drawing*).
Come on! *My* sword's drawn –

ALBA (*unmoved*).
Do you know what to do with it?

CARLOS.
Try me. You see my sword –

ALBA.
I see no man to manage it –

CARLOS.
Draw, or I'll kill you –

ALBA.
Heaven sees it's not my doing –

*They fight furiously. The doors of ELIZABETH's apartment
are thrown open. Enter GUARDS who stop the fight,
OLIVAREZ, DOMINGO, then ELIZABETH.*

ELIZABETH.
Carlos!

*Shocked by her appearance, CARLOS lets his arm fall,
then rushes to ALBA and kisses him.*

CARLOS.
The kiss of peace, Alba.
You're leaving Spain – let's not part in anger.
Spain's Prince forgives you all your trespasses
in love and charity – Farewell.

*He suddenly throws himself at ELIZABETH's feet. Kisses
her hand very formally, backs, then hurries away. ALBA,
astonished, bows low to her. ELIZABETH retreats into her
rooms with OLIVAREZ. DOMINGO remains with ALBA.
The GUARDS go in and shut the doors.*

ALBA.
I could almost think . . .
Did you see, Domingo,
the lingering look she gave him?
Did you note its effect?

A single, imperious look –
yet, somehow – *intimate*?

DOMINGO.
Is it not suspicious, Duke?
I'd say so.
Come with me, I've things to say to you.

Scene Eight

A secret rendezvous in a private chapel. RODRIGO *is waiting impatiently.* CARLOS *enters, still in a fever of excitement.*

RODRIGO.
Do you know how long I've been waiting?

CARLOS.
It doesn't matter – nothing matters –

RODRIGO.
You've made your peace?

CARLOS.
With whom?

RODRIGO.
With the King – your father? –

CARLOS.
O my father! –

RODRIGO.
Flanders! – is it decided?

CARLOS.
Yes –

RODRIGO.
Thank God! You're going to Flanders?

CARLOS.
Alba's to be Viceroy –

RODRIGO.
  It's not true! The news from Court –
  There are people on the streets of Madrid
  cheering your appointment –

CARLOS.
  Their celebration's premature –

RODRIGO.
  No! –

CARLOS.
  Alba marches within the week –

RODRIGO.
  Your father refused you? –

CARLOS.
  Yes! Yes! Yes!
  It's of no consequence – Listen to me, Rodrigo.
  I have to see the Queen –
  There is still hope for us – but you must advise me –

RODRIGO.
  What hope? –

CARLOS.
  My heart – my love – depends upon it –
  I must speak to her –

RODRIGO.
  We're lost –

CARLOS.
  Look!
  Listen to me!
  This – it's from the King – see – his handwriting –

RODRIGO (*reading it*).
  To? – What's –

CARLOS.
  To the Princess Eboli.
  She confessed everything to me – opened her heart –
  She knows I am in love –
  but she thought it was with her –

RODRIGO.
Eboli?

CARLOS.
Poor soul! – *She's* my father's guilty secret!
And she's asked my protection –

RODRIGO.
Eboli's in love with you?

CARLOS.
No – not any longer. She knows her love's not returned –

RODRIGO.
She knows! –
Has she guessed whom you really love?

CARLOS.
No!

RODRIGO.
Of course she has! – O she's solved the riddle!
Carlos – what have you done?
Think, man! You've rejected her – she knows your secret –
and now you're at her mercy!
What possessed you!

CARLOS.
We've nothing to fear. She's an innocent – she loved me –

RODRIGO.
Loved – loved! She *offered* herself to you –

CARLOS (*snatching back the letter*).
Yes! She did.

RODRIGO.
And you refused her.
I fear – I fear –

CARLOS.
She'll never betray me – you don't know her –

RODRIGO.
I know her well enough.
I know she wears her seeming virtue like a mask –
carries pride in her blood like a hidden dagger.

Her hopes of you must have lifted her high –
Rejected, insulted, wounded – now she'll fall.
And in falling she'll try and pull you down.
She may strike at the Queen too –
You've placed Elizabeth in danger –

CARLOS (*angry*).
    Never! Never! I'll speak to Elizabeth.

RODRIGO.
    And tell her what?
    (*Horrified realisation.*) You don't intend to show her this?

CARLOS.
    I do.
    This frees her of her husband – me of my father – both of
    us – free!
    What have we left to lose?

RODRIGO.
    You say you love her – this may destroy her.
    Do you think she'll read it with joy?
    Will it make her happy?
    Look at me.
    Swear you're doing this out of love for her?

    CARLOS, *ashamed, cannot look* RODRIGO *in the eye. He
    looks at the ground and is silent.*

    Here's something I've not seen before –
    something furtive – unlovable –
    Don't turn away. Can't you look me in the eye?
    Give it to me.

    CARLOS *hands over the letter.*

    Say your father's a liar, a hypocrite, an adulterer –
    does that mean he's no longer a danger? –
    to you, to the wife he wrongs,
    to the cause we're fighting for? –
    A cause you've abandoned.
    So now you know your father's not a saint.
    And you –
    O how deceived I've been in you!

RODRIGO *destroys the letter.*

CARLOS.
Rodrigo –

RODRIGO.
You used to have a soul so great
the world might turn upon its axis
and never leave the confines of your heart.
Now I find you spineless, gutless –
All that compassion – infinite compassion –
shrunk and shrivelled into this single, destructive *self.*
A fire is raging in your heart – burning you away to
nothing.
All that's left are the cold ashes of my hopes.

CARLOS (*in tears, he tries to hide them from* RODRIGO).
I've lost you too.

RODRIGO.
Carlos.
Understand.
Without each other we are nothing. (*Embraces* CARLOS.)
You're suffering, but – believe me, Carlos –
good will grow from it.
You've lost your way.
Let's search our hearts – find out our weaknesses to know
our strengths.
And, yes – there is no other way – you must speak to the
Queen,
and so must I.
You'll trust from her
what you will not accept from me.

CARLOS (*kneels to him*).
I am shamed by your humanity –

RODRIGO.
Kneel to nobody –
be the Prince you are. (*Lifting him up.*)
There's a glimmer of hope – an idea –
No, first I must speak to her.
There is a way . . .

A mass begins. CARLOS *and* RODRIGO *lower their voices.*

We to whom God entrusts his works
must offer ourselves in the service of the weak,
the oppressed, and the powerless.
And if we catch ourselves failing – again and again –
and even if our failure brings us to the utmost point of despair,
from somewhere we must find the strength
to endure – to go forward – and to keep faith.

CARLOS.
Our strength is in each other.

RODRIGO *kneels and kisses* CARLOS' *hand.*

RODRIGO.
Once more the loyal servant and the Prince.

CARLOS.
A warning, Rodrigo:
do you communicate with our friends in Flanders?

RODRIGO.
Every day.

CARLOS.
Be vigilant.
All letters to and from Flanders
are scrutinised by Count Cordua
and shown to my father.

RODRIGO.
I know.
I am no novice in these affairs.

This reply puzzles CARLOS. *Exeunt separately.*

Scene Nine

PRINCESS EBOLI *comes out of a confessional in confusion, followed immediately by* DOMINGO.

DOMINGO.
> You owe me the truth!
> My lady, the truth!
> Your confessor must know what's in your heart.

EBOLI.
> You delivered the King my former answer? –

DOMINGO.
> No, lady – I did not.

EBOLI.
> Why? Why –

DOMINGO.
> Bluntly, I did not know how to sugar so bitter a pill.

> *Slight pause.*

> Great kings are unaccustomed to rejection.
> Refusal makes them doubt themselves.
> What good's a king who doubts himself?
> Spain's King gives all freely –
> For Spain to ask some slight return . . .

> Let me speak plainly:
> To refuse King Philip may seem in you, his subject,
> uncharitable – even culpable.

EBOLI.
> Some slight return –

DOMINGO.
> Believe me – I understand.
> A woman's pride requires – demands –
> some show of resistance.
> But mellowing time softens the hardest of hearts.
> Think of the honour – think what you'd gain.

EBOLI.

Reverend sir,

you may tell His Majesty I'll be his whore.

DOMINGO.

Such language! Remember where you are!

Slight pause.

Dare I believe it?

EBOLI.

You think I'd answer lightly?

Oh, oh – what's this, what's this? – turning pale?

Have I shamed you? –

Even you – the man whose

trade is Spain's most shameful secrets? –

Am I then so terrible?

DOMINGO.

What surprises me is not this change of heart – this

commendable change –

but its suddenness.

EBOLI.

No change in me.

Others change . . . Times change.

I rebuffed King Philip's lewd proposals –

I was troubled, then . . .

thinking of his sacred marriage vows.

I remembered the honour of my lady, the Queen

whom I thought constant – faithful.

DOMINGO.

Go on.

EBOLI.

I thought her worth my loyalty.

Now *there's* the change.

DOMINGO.

Go on.

Reluctant to confess her secrets?

Don't be afraid.

I was about to reveal them to you.
I know everything.

EBOLI.

Then I need conceal nothing.
She's in love.
I know she is in love.
With –

DOMINGO.

With Don Carlos – yes.
She's a traitor to the King – to Spain –

EBOLI.

An adulteress!
I know it for a fact –

DOMINGO.

And the son plots treason with her against his father.
I need evidence –

EBOLI.

I'll bring you evidence –
proof to shake the State,
and break her crown in pieces.

DOMINGO.

Bring me *written* evidence.
Do letters pass between them?
You have access to the Queen's apartments –
caskets? Keys?
Are her servants true?
I suppose you know –
Gold can do much where loyalty guards the door.

EBOLI.

Leave everything to me.

DOMINGO.

And Don Carlos –
In whom does our gloomy Prince confide? –

EBOLI (*too quickly*).

No one.
He has no friend –

DOMINGO.

> Sure?
> The Queen's page handed him a letter –

EBOLI.

> That was nothing –
> another matter –

DOMINGO.

> But –

EBOLI.

> I know about that – it was nothing.
> Nothing.

DOMINGO (*guessing the whole thing*).

> Ah . . .
> What shall I tell the King?

EBOLI.

> In a few days my monthly sickness is due.
> Custom requires me to keep my rooms.
> Tell him that.

DOMINGO.

> Te absolvo. The peace of God go with you.

> *She exits.* ALBA *comes out of* DOMINGO's *side of the
> confessional.*

> She came to tell us what we've guessed already.
> What's to become of us, Duke, what's to become of us
> when this dangerous young man becomes our king?
> I fear for the Church.
> I fear for the throne.

ALBA.

> I fear for our influence over both of them.
> But what can we do?
> Let's hope the grind of government will force him to
> conform –
> Young rulers are all the same:
> before they get power they're full of projects and promises –
> afterwards – well, the drudgery of it all
> makes them draw in their horns.

DOMINGO.

I'm not so sure.
Could you control Carlos once he's seized the Crown?
I know I couldn't – believe me, I've tried.
There are no chinks in his armour – girls, boys . . .
God made me 'a fisher of men' but I've failed to hook this one.
No, no – I'm afraid our heir to the throne
is virtuous, honourable – a visionary sort of youth.
And if he joins forces with the Queen, we're lost.
Elizabeth and Carlos were cast in the same mould –
Reformers, innovators, both overfull of zeal.
They have contracted the same terrible disease: *Humanity.*
And Humanity, you know, is very contagious.
What I would call pride in them – over-reaching, and self-love –
they would call freedom of conscience – and benevolence.
The throne of Spain could fall victim to either one,
but if the two of them join forces . . .
Well, where are we then, Duke of Alba?

ALBA.

What can we do?

DOMINGO.

We must try the power of prayer.

Or strike them down –
Two birds with one stone – two rats in a single trap.
Just a hint to the King that they're plotting against him –
that they're at it in his bed –

ALBA.

But what if they're not?
What if it's Eboli's jealous fantasy?
Who knows the workings of a woman's mind?

DOMINGO.

I do, Duke. I'm her confessor –
What does it matter if it's true or false? –
So long as it buys us *time.*
We shall discover more – and worse –
Trust to it.

ALBA.

> But now the hardest thing of all:
> Which of us dare whisper this to the King?

DOMINGO.

> Neither of us.
> The Princess Eboli shall be our tale-bearer.
> His Majesty's besotted with her –
> I know this – I'm his confessor.
> I've fanned the flames of his lust,
> and from the first sparks of it I've played the royal pander.
> What's the matter?

ALBA.

> I'm waiting for Him to strike us dead!

DOMINGO.

> Who?

ALBA.

> Almighty God the Father.

DOMINGO.

> But He won't, Duke, He won't.
> Not while we're about His business.

ACT THREE

Scene Ten

A week later. KING PHILIP's bed-chamber. Almost dawn – in night-shirt and dressing gown, PHILIP sits at the small table half asleep. On the table is a small pile of personal letters – stolen by PRINCESS EBOLI from QUEEN ELIZABETH, written by CARLOS. PHILIP holds in one hand a miniature portrait of CARLOS on a gold chain. PHILIP has been studying it intently but he is no longer aware that he is holding it. In his other hand he holds a letter. His grip relaxes and the letter falls from his hand onto the table. He half wakes.

PHILIP.
There is a wildness in Elizabeth's soul –
she's untameable – free.
I have never loved. Am I incapable of love?
Did she expect love of me? – or ever ask it?
And now they tell me she's false . . . Here –
this letter, they say, is proof of it.

Picks up the letter and tries to concentrate on it but his eyes keep closing.

The lights burn low. Day will not dawn . . .
I dare not close my eyes.

CARLOS' portrait falls from his hand onto the table, waking him. He rings a bell and shouts:

Lerma! Lerma!

He goes to the window and looks out.

My subjects – all asleep . . .
Duty sleeps – no longer in awe of majesty –
How am I then a king?

PHILIP hides the letters under a portfolio as LERMA comes in. LERMA is shocked by PHILIP's appearance.

LERMA.

Sire – are you unwell? Were you unable to sleep?

PHILIP.

Sleep? They're building me a tomb in the Escorial – when
it's finished, I'll sleep.
For now . . .

He cannot resist a glance at the letters.

(*To himself.*) While the King sleeps
the knave steals his crown –
while the old man sleeps
the young men labour with his wife.

I cannot believe it. I'll never, never believe it.

Pushes away the letters.

A woman brought me these.
Shall I let women's tales unman me? –
No! It's worthless gossip.
I lack proof positive – I'll have it confirmed before . . .

Rings bell and calls off.

Boy! Go and wake up the Duke of Alba.

LERMA (*concerned*).

Sire –

PHILIP.

What do you think, Lerma?
Oh to make windows into their souls!
Tell me the truth – are all about me loyal?
Is it true? – Is it?

LERMA.

Your Majesty –

PHILIP.

Majesty! Majesty! Always, always, Majesty!
I thirst for friendly counsel – you offer me liquid gold!

LERMA.

What truth do you speak of, my lord!
What do you want of me?

PHILIP.

Nothing! Nothing. Leave me. Go.

LERMA *bows and makes to leave.*

Lerma.

LERMA *turns.*

I've not slept.
My mind's still wandering in a world of dreams –
nightmares –
It's nothing – forget what you've heard.
You understand me?
Your King is well pleased with your loyal service.

He holds out his hand for LERMA *to kiss – which he does,
gratefully, then exits.* PHILIP *cannot resist pulling the
offending letters towards him and reading them over again.*
ALBA *enters, sleepy, worried.*

ALBA.

Forgive me, Majesty –
It's very early –

PHILIP *silences him with an angry look. He studies* ALBA
for a long time, still in silence.

PHILIP.

You've betrayed me.

ALBA.

Majesty! –

PHILIP.

All of you.
There's a knife in my heart –
You saw the blow coming – and you looked the other way –

ALBA.

Majesty –

PHILIP.

Traitors.
Whose writing is this?

ALBA.
It is Don Carlos' hand –

He's trembling.

PHILIP.
You warned me he was dangerous – ambitious –
'He must not go unwatched.' – Remember?

ALBA.
What has –

PHILIP.
'He must not go unwatched.'
Well?
Have you been watchful?

ALBA.
I have . . . but –

PHILIP.
Read it.

ALBA *reads* CARLOS' *letter.*

ALBA.
I cannot think . . .
Who brought you this, Sire? –
To write so openly to her –

PHILIP.
To her? To her? You know then to whom he writes? –

ALBA.
I –

PHILIP.
How do you know? When the letter's not addressed?

ALBA.
I –

PHILIP.
How?

ALBA.
Majesty.
Nothing is proven – But as I guess . . . I . . .

PHILIP.

As you guess? – No, liar – You *know*!

ALBA.

He's writing to the Queen!

PHILIP.

To my wife. His mother. Dear God!
In all my boundless Empire
am I the last to know?

ALBA.

Majesty!
The guilt upon my head –

PHILIP *strikes him to his knees.*

I am shamed.
How could I speak out?
Your son . . . your wife . . .
Love of the honour of my King –
Where could I begin?
Duty, truth, the good of the State thundered in my ears for
justice –
but to accuse your son – your wife . . .
How could I speak ill of those my sovereign loves?

PHILIP.

Cunning dog!
Speak now. Get up.

ALBA.

The evidence is not conclusive –

PHILIP *rages.*

PHILIP.

Get out! Leave me!

ALBA *starts to go.*

God grant me one loyal subject
one who dare speak to me like a man!
Is this conclusive? (*Throwing a letter at* ALBA.)
Is this? (*Another.*) Is this?

He is about to throw the portrait of his son, but stops and
studies it. Then holds it against his own miniature of the
QUEEN *which he wears on a gold chain about his neck.*

Their guilt shines clearer than the sun at noon . . .
I've always suspected – always known.
I saw it first at daybreak when she came to me,
arrayed in the shining beauty of a young bride, all smiles.
My son was standing at my side – I saw – she could not
hide it –
a moment of wide-eyed horror.
She saw me . . . Grey.
The colour in her cheeks
drained to a ghostly white . . .
She glanced at Carlos – she fell in love.

ALBA.
   Majesty.
   In the vanity of their imagination
   they were already lovers –
   each promised to the other –
   Then, out of care for the State, you took the Prince's bride
   and gave him, in her place, a mother.
   The Princess came in search of love
   and found instead crowns and thrones –

PHILIP
   I applaud your honesty,
   welcome your directness. (*Insulted and with bitterness.*)
   The Emperor thanks the Duke of Alba
   for forcing this bitter remembrance into his ears.
   (*Rings the bell and calls off.*) Fetch the Dominican.

ALBA.
   If I have given offence, Majesty
   it is only through diligence and –

PHILIP.
   You're dismissed. Go.

ALBA (*bowing low*).
   Majesty.

PHILIP (*not harshly*).
God made you what you are.
I must forgive you for it.

Exit ALBA.

Heaven send me a man I can trust –

*He opens a book in which the qualities and crimes of his
courtiers are listed and begins to run his finger down the
list, then breaks off and prays:*

Oh God my Saviour –
You've given me sovereignty – kingdoms in abundance –
now bless me with a good man – a friend, a counsellor,
to guide me in their government.
I ask it only for Thy greater glory.

Enter DOMINGO.

DOMINGO.
Now God be thanked!
Your Majesty remains steadfast – so calm.

PHILIP.
Should I not be calm?

DOMINGO.
I feared these revelations –

PHILIP.
What do you know of revelations?

DOMINGO.
Forgive me.
All I dare say, Majesty, is that I have heard of secrets –
terrible secrets –

PHILIP.
You presume too far.
Have I asked your counsel?

DOMINGO.
Believe me, Majesty,
I do not raise such matters lightly –
Yet when the secrets of the confessional,

touch both the security of the State,
and the safety of God's deputy on Earth –
I hope I know my duty.

After a moment's pause PHILIP *motions him to proceed.*

The Princess Eboli, Majesty, has confessed to me –
sins that have weighed heavily upon her tender soul.
Yet knowing that confession and repentance
would entangle the honour of her Royal Mistress –

PHILIP.
The Princess Eboli has a simple heart.
She was not made for intrigue.

DOMINGO.
What good can come of scandal, Majesty?
Why bring to light faults that may blemish
the Queen's honour
and wound your own?
I would advise – may I?

PHILIP *nods.*

Best leave all dark.
The favour of kings obscures all error.
The frown of kings silences rumour.

PHILIP.
Rumour? Among my people?

DOMINGO.
Lies!
Alas! Alas! I fear the Queen's good name has become a
theme for idle tongues –
the merchandise of all the city trades –

PHILIP.
Who would dare –

DOMINGO.
Madrid's a sink of scandal –

PHILIP.
What are they saying? Tell me – quickly! –

DOMINGO.

Nothing that's true –

PHILIP.

God give me patience! Must I beg scorpions to sting my
ears –

DOMINGO.

There's a calumny in Madrid – without foundation – believe
me, I know the truth –
that Your Majesty's daughter –

PHILIP.

Tread softly –

DOMINGO.

Is not your own.

PHILIP *controls himself with difficulty.*

Thirty weeks before her birth –
or so the rumour runs – Your Majesty
was grievously sick –

PHILIP.

Alba! Alba! Where is my sword – my guards!
Alba! –

ALBA, LERMA, PAGES *and* GUARDS *burst in* – ALBA
with sword drawn.

As you are a man, protect me from this sexless thing – this
obscenity – this priest!

ALBA *doesn't know what to do.* LERMA, *sensing the
situation – he thinks* PHILIP *is out of his mind from lack of
sleep, hurries out the others.*

DOMINGO.

You wrung it from me, Majesty!
I am the innocent bearer of these guilty tales –

PHILIP.

My daughter's mine! Who dare say otherwise!

DOMINGO.

Would you rather I shut my ears – my mouth –

ALBA.

You mistake us, Majesty! –

PHILIP.

Us? –

ALBA.

Our love and loyalty –

PHILIP.

Us!

Oh I've caught you out! Here's conspiracy! –
Your fawning innocence is well rehearsed –
But I see there's been collusion here!

DOMINGO.

No! –

ALBA.

You wrong us –

PHILIP.

Do I? Do I?
But what could you hope to gain?
You'd have the glories I've denied my son –
You, a kennel in Rome –
and what, for me, are the fruits of your love and loyalty?
Answer!
To doubt my wife, my son – and lose for ever quietness of
mind?
Oh no – I've seen you at work!
(*To* ALBA.) You drip in the poison that will stop my heart!
(*To* DOMINGO.) You'd smooth my way down the road to Hell
and abandon me at the gates!
Well, since you plant doubts in me
let their first flowering be doubts of your own loyalty.
Show me your proofs!

DOMINGO.

Majesty, you have the letters Don Carlos wrote.
That's proof of their love.
You have the Princess Eboli's suspicions,
that's proof of adultery.

What stronger witness could there be?
Unless you found them in your bed?

PHILIP.

You've said enough.
Lerma! Assemble my lords in council –
I myself will sit in judgement on my wife and son,
and you, their accusers, will plead your case against them.
If you prove the Queen adulterous she'll suffer . . .
The Crown Prince with her.
But if you fail – if they're found innocent – the fire you
build for them's your own.

DOMINGO *kneels in fear.*

Now what do you say?
Will you risk your lives to prove what's false true?
What's your answer?
Dumbstruck? Nothing to say now?
This hesitation shows you cowards, liars –

ALBA.

I'll do it.

PHILIP, *astonished, stares at* ALBA *for a while. Then sees
through him.*

PHILIP.

Out of bravado. Not bravery –
You're a cornered rat going for the throat –
a soldier, a dicer, Alba –
gambling your life for a moment's bluster.
Your sacrifice is worthless to me –
your soul too light to be weighed in the balance against the
blood royal.
The stake's too low. I'll not accept your bet.
Out. Get out.

Exeunt ALBA *and* DOMINGO. PHILIP *goes back to the book.*

Dear God, why do You shackle me with *politicians*? –
Spiritless – vengeful – evil –
they've worn their souls to rags and tatters
toiling up the rocky paths to self-regard –
None of them any use to me . . .

Lord, answer my prayers!
I need the healing balm of friendship.
I need a man whose heart's unwritten –
whose soul is pure.
I need a man of vision
to lead me in new ways to truth.

Lerma!

LERMA.
Majesty?

PHILIP.
That young man
Who came to us in Aranjuez –
the traveller –

LERMA.
The Marquis of Posa?

PHILIP (*looking through his book*).
Posa? I've no recollection of him.
[Black marks, recorded crimes, few notes of merit –
Retribution's more diligent than reward –
that's bad, bad –

Posa? Posa. Here –
In my book I've underlined his name. Twice.
That means I once marked him down for high office –
Is it possible?
Why have I neglected him? Where has he been?
I can hardly recall his face or voice.] *
Why doesn't he ask our royal favour? –
beg for preferment like all the others.

LERMA.
He's a good man, Majesty, and a brave one,
but free-spirited and a little proud.

PHILIP.
Go – fetch him here.

Exit LERMA.

* The bracketed speech was omitted from the Sheffield Crucible production.

Is this my answer, God?
A free-spirit and a little proud? It's what I need –
a brave man – untainted by the temptations of office
free of the corrupting customs of the court –
A pure, clear voice – a new beginning.
I'll try him, test him – pray he's my salvation.
Only God can see the truth of a man;
only Truth can cure my sickly State – restore my peace of
mind, and bring me sleep, sleep, sleep . . .

Scene Eleven

[*In the Sheffield Crucible production, the Court sequence with
the Duke of Medina Sidonia was transposed to the beginning
of this scene. In this published text it begins at the bottom of
page 80.*]

KING PHILIP *is sitting at his desk reading and signing
documents which* LERMA *seals.* RODRIGO, *in his best Court
dress, wearing his cross – the Order of the Knights of Malta –
around his neck and on his cloak, stands downstage, waiting.
Occasionally* PHILIP *glances at him.*

PHILIP.
All lost? All?
It's God's will. (*Crosses himself.*)

LERMA *bows low and exits with the documents.* PHILIP
consults his book of names then looks at RODRIGO.

You've never before been granted an audience?

RODRIGO.
No.

PHILIP.
You fought bravely at Valetta (*Consulting the book.*)
'when the fortress was besieged by
Suleiman's army . . . and earned your cross.'
You were eighteen years old.
Let's see –

'The Marquis of Posa unmasked the conspiracy in Catalonia
preserving that province for the Crown of Spain.'
Yet you've never drawn attention to your merit –
as was your duty.
Why not, young man?

RODRIGO.
I've only recently returned to Court.

PHILIP.
It is not the custom
for kings of Spain to be beholden to their subjects.
And this King . . . is very jealous of his honour.
How may Spain reward you?

RODRIGO.
Duty expects no reward.

PHILIP.
Yet ask.

RODRIGO.
I enjoy the benefits of a country at peace –
The protection of the law –

PHILIP.
Murderers – thieves – *heretics* . . . could say the same.

RODRIGO.
But an honest man enjoys the quiet mind
that peace and justice brings.
I hope I'm honest –

PHILIP.
Is this humility or is it arrogance?
Well, arrogance is forgivable in a Spaniard.
You don't wish to serve me?

RODRIGO.
You have better men than me.
I would not wish to keep a better man down.

PHILIP.
Service is beneath you?

RODRIGO.

No, Majesty! I am sensible of the honour –
But . . .

PHILIP.

Go on.

RODRIGO.

I do not choose to offer myself to you.

I'm not for hire – not worth the market price.
Yes – I wish to serve
but my service is for my fellow men,
and to serve them I need my freedom.
I wish to build, to create –

PHILIP.

Create what? A better world?

RODRIGO.

Yes –

PHILIP.

So do I. Why else would God have set me on this Earth?

Slight pause.

You wish to do good – I have the power to grant that wish.
Name any office in my Empire –

RODRIGO.

There isn't one.

PHILIP.

You're wrong.

RODRIGO.

Your Majesty, I'm not wrong.
You serve God –
I serve him too – I believe I have much to offer humanity –
But what I call service
you would condemn as freedom of conscience.

PHILIP *looks astonished.*

Great kings distribute the abundance of their empires –
lift up their favourites, reward their servants,

honour their subjects' loyalty. Good gifts? Yes.
But the gold kings give is stamped with the king's image
and must be repaid – in servility, faith, and unquestioning
obedience.
You'd stamp your head on mine.
I'd fill men's heads with dreams of freedom,
teach them to question everything,
show them where to find their own blessings –

PHILIP.

Are we speaking of revolution, or of heresy?

RODRIGO.

Sire, you know as well as I
there's great corruption in our Roman Church
but I've not abandoned her. Not yet.

Don't misinterpret me.
I am no rebel – no Samson –
let's not pull down the temple on our heads.
I don't question men's faith – I'm no threat to your crown –
I accept the need for kings – but I no longer fear them.
My dream is of the future – a heaven on earth –
a time when we'll have no use for sovereignty . . .
A time neither of us will live to see.
For the present, I kneel before your throne.
A poor man's dreams can't hurt you.

PHILIP.

Have you told these dreams to anyone else?
Am I the first to see into your soul?

RODRIGO.

Yes.

PHILIP *comes down to* RODRIGO *and looks hard into his
eyes.*

PHILIP.

Are they only dreams? Keep them from the Inquisition.
Are you merely another flatterer, more cunning than the
rest, or the answer to my prayers?
One thing you've proved already –
I can still be surprised.

I like to be surprised –
surprised there's still some good in men.
Surely I can find a way to curb your stubbornness –
to harness your independent spirit and use it for our
country's good.
Be my conscience.
Challenge my casual authority!
Be my opposition!

RODRIGO.
No.
I've told you my mind –
still you suspect my real aim is employment.
And who could blame you?
All courtiers feed upon their king – gobble up his favours –
abandon dignity – nobility – for the scraps from his table.
Willing slaves, they thrust their necks beneath your foot . . .
So now you think all men the same.
Is it any wonder that you treat such
botched and patched humanity
with contempt?

PHILIP.
I can't deny the truth of that.

RODRIGO.
God gave you subjects to rule –
You remould them in your own image.
Remember this – you're not a god.
You're human – with human failings, human needs.
You go among your people like a petty deity
but you suffer like a man.
You are feared, but you're not loved.

PHILIP (to himself).
His gentle truth will break my heart.

RODRIGO.
What can your wretched people offer back to you?
They possess nothing you value – nothing you desire –
nothing that's not already yours.
When mens' imaginations are made to conform –
when every varied action or impulse is crushed by custom –

where will you find invention, originality, progress?
If you snuff out freedom of conscience – freedom of
thought –
how can the world move closer to Heaven?
You say you wish to do good? Create a better world?
Think, Majesty – before you throw away
the very thing you're searching for.
Truth's the richest prize of all . . .

Dismiss me.
I've said too much –
and nothing I say can help you.

PHILIP.
Let me be judge of that.
This truth – this prize –
I see you are burning to speak out.
So . . . I'm listening.

RODRIGO.
Very well.
I've just come home from Flanders –

PHILIP.
I don't choose to discuss Flanders! I forbid you to –

RODRIGO.
The beating heart of your rich Empire –
A mighty people noble and upright.
To be king of such a nation, I thought,
is something of worth . . .
But then I saw your Inquisition at work –
the acrid stench of burning human flesh –
the twisted heaps of blackened bones.

He falls silent, looking into PHILIP's *eyes.* PHILIP *tries to
return his gaze, but can't. Ashamed, he lowers his eyes to
the floor.*

I know what you'll say:
You must defend our faith.
It's God's work you're doing.

That you have a heart cold enough to let it happen
chills my own – I offer you my icy respect.

O shame, that your victims – smothering in their blood –
can't believe you're acting for the good of their souls!
O shame, that in the gentler age to come
history may mistake your stewardship for tyranny.

PHILIP.
There will be no gentler age –
If I don't find the courage to burn out the heresies of our own.
Look about!
My Spain! I've given her a lasting peace.
My people thrive!
No clouds on their horizon!
And such a peace I'll bring to Flanders.

RODRIGO.
Who, in Flanders, will live to enjoy it?
Their faith in Christ seeks to renew itself and grow strong.
You'll send a winter to freeze their spring –
floods to drown their harvests.
But you'll not stop them –
You can't imprison men's minds –
You'll never do it –
You're driving out your best, most industrious subjects –
thousands have fled to Elizabeth of England –
more will follow –
Here in Madrid, men who tell the truth
are hounded to the fires –
You strike at your own people, and your enemies rejoice.

PHILIP *is deeply moved.* RODRIGO *sees this and moves
closer to him – pressing home his point.*

You wish to plant a garden that will flower for ever.
Why do you water it with blood?
Yet . . .
I cannot believe you're unmoved by suffering –
You were once your people's hope – a good prince to them –

PHILIP (*suspecting flattery*).
Was I?

RODRIGO.
God knows you were! (*With heat.*)

Yes – yes – I say you were!
Come back to your people – give us back our hope.
A single word of yours
could set the world upon its proper course.
Give men the freedom to think and speak –
unchain their tongues and they'll use them to rejoice.
A million voices praying for their king's happiness –
Isn't that better than grudging praise enforced by terror?

He kneels. PHILIP, *overcome, turns his face away.*

PHILIP.
Dreamer . . . Stand up.

RODRIGO.
You're afraid.
The mightiest king in Christendom
fears the imagination of a few thinking men.

PHILIP.
Stand up.

RODRIGO *stands.*

I will not punish you.
I see there's honesty in your words – and in your manner.
I'll answer you – not as your king
but as an older, wiser man.
Beware my Inquisition.
I should be sorry . . .
if –

RODRIGO.
Sorry? –

PHILIP.
I would not lose you.

RODRIGO.
You've lost better.
Flanders has a thousand better men.
I've known –

PHILIP.
I never knew them!

I never looked into their eyes.

We'll go no further with this.
Brave young man – when you've lived in the world –
sifted men as I have done –
If you could look into the truth of things –
If you had been forced
to face horrors youth could never imagine –
Then you'll know me as I am – just another slave of terrible
necessity.
I say I would not lose you.
What shall I do – tell me how may I bind you to me?

RODRIGO.

Leave me as I am – offer me nothing.
If you corrupt me, I'll be as worthless
as all your other flatterers –

PHILIP.

I let you speak freely and it makes you proud.
Let me advise you – curb that pride, sir.
I take you into my service – as of this moment –
Denial is useless – my mind's made up.
The King wishes it!

Pause.

A free spirit, and fearless – well . . . it's what I prayed for.

Rings the bell. LERMA *enters;* PHILIP *gives* RODRIGO
his hand to kiss.

Lerma, you may call them in.
This knight may be admitted to the presence whenever he
wishes.
Unannounced.
Come with me.

PHILIP *leads* RODRIGO *into the inner office.* LERMA *lets
in the* COUNCILLORS *including* ALBA, DOMINGO, *and
any others, all with documents and petitions. Pre-meeting
atmosphere.* CARLOS *comes in, deep in conversation with
his teenage cousin, the* PRINCE OF PARMA. ALBA *avoids*

him. Finally, MEDINA SIDONIA, *Admiral of the
Fleet, comes in, all turn their backs on him, except*
CARLOS *who doesn't see him.* MEDINA SIDONIA
approaches ALBA.

MEDINA SIDONIA.
Alba – have you spoken to His Majesty?

ALBA.
I have.

MEDINA SIDONIA.
What's his mood?

ALBA.
Cold. I'd say your presence here in Court
is as unwelcome to him,
as the news you bring.

MEDINA SIDONIA.
Dear God, I'd rather face the English in the Channel
than the frown of my king.

CARLOS, *aware of his distress, comes up with* PARMA
and offers his hand.

CARLOS.
Prince of Parma,
May I present Don Alonzo Perez de Guzmán,
Duke of Medina Sidonia,
Lord Admiral of the Fleet.

MEDINA SIDONIA (*low bows*).
My Princes,
this kindly gesture means more to me than I can say.
You see how the others shun me.
Greatness toppled from favour
finds few companions in its fall.

CARLOS.
The King's not vengeful, Admiral –
and you were not to blame.
Hope for the best.
Always hope for the best.

MEDINA SIDONIA.

>What right have I to hope?
>Have I not lost the greatest fleet that ever sailed?
>What's this poor head worth – weighed in the balance
>against seventy proud ships wrecked on the Irish shore
>with all the fiery youth of Spain?
>I have five sons, eager to serve their country.
>Now, my disgrace will ruin them all –
>How can I bear to look them in the eye?

>PHILIP, *formally robed, comes out of the inner office. All
>take off their hats.*

PHILIP.

>Cover!

>*His glance at* MEDINA SIDONIA *gives nothing away.*

>CARLOS *and the* PRINCE OF PARMA *do not cover but
>are the first to go and kiss* PHILIP*'s hand. The rest put on
>their hats. Concealing his feelings with difficulty,* PHILIP
>*receives* CARLOS *very coldly, but smiles warmly on young*
>PARMA.

>Dear child – nephew.
>Your mother has written to me –
>she's eager to know what impression you're making in
>Madrid.

PARMA.

>Mothers!
>Majesty, let her wait until I've fought my first battle –
>then she'll hear how I'll teach the world my name.

PHILIP.

>You will, you will.
>For now, be patient.
>When this dead wood is swept away

>*Looking at his commanders.*

>I'll give you armies to command.

>What's the business of the day?

LERMA.
> The Grand Master of the Order of Knights of Calatrava
> is on the point of death.

> *All cross themselves.*

> He returns to Your Majesty, his cross. (*Presents it.*)

PHILIP.
> Who is worthiest to succeed him?

> *He looks around.* ALBA *expects it.*

> I'll give it thought. (*Gives the cross back to* LERMA.)
> Admiral?

MEDINA SIDONIA (*goes and kneels at* PHILIP*'s feet*).
> Behold in me, Majesty,
> the sad remains of your youthful soldiery –
> a poor survivor of your mighty fleet.

PHILIP (*after a long pause*).
> The Heavens are above our heads.
> I sent you to fight Englishmen,
> not storms and raging seas.
> You are welcome home to Madrid.

> *Gives him his hand to kiss.*

> And I thank God for your safe return.
> The Crown has great need of good men –
> and I count you among my best.
> Lords, show him honour.

> CARLOS *and* PARMA *lead* MEDINA SIDONIA *aside.*
> *The* LORDS *bow to him.*

> (*To* CARLOS *and* PARMA.) Princes,
> I thank you both.
> You have leave to go.

> CARLOS *and* PARMA *bow out with* MEDINA SIDONIA.

> Who can tell us something of the Marquis of Posa?
> We're informed he's brave – a man of integrity.
> Why does he not present himself at Court?

DOMINGO.

> Majesty, the Marquis Posa has only in these last few days
> returned to Madrid.
> He's been a traveller – welcomed in all the Courts of
> Europe –
> valued for his manners, and nobleness of mind.
> I'm sure he will present himself,
> showing his duty, when the Court summons him.

ALBA.

> He's a fighter too –
> Remember that business at the siege of Malta? –
> And he risked his life in Catalonia,
> double-dealing to entrap the conspirators.

PHILIP.

> A sound man, then?

ALL.

> Yes, Your Majesty.

PHILIP.

> My lords, you astonish me!
> Not one of you has a word to speak against him –
> this Marquis of Posa?
> What's happened to your customary back-biting?
> Where is envy, jealousy, family pride, mistrust?
> Is he so highly thought of to be above reproach?
> Or so low, as to be beneath your notice?
> In either case it's a miracle –
> You'll all go to Mass and thank God for it.
> Lerma, we must grant the Marquis an audience.

> [(*Aside to* LERMA.) It seems I've chosen well.

Exeunt. RODRIGO *comes out of the inner office.*

RODRIGO.

> Why me? It cannot be accident – cannot be unplanned.
> What force or trick of destiny has placed me here
> inside the very heart of government?
> Are these my hands – Do I stand here?
> Within this little room the fate of nations is determined.
> Again, I ask – Dear God –

what angel – or devil – prompted the memory of the King
to summon me – of all his subjects?
But then – what does it matter?
What he plans to do with me's of little consequence.
What matters is what I shall do with him –
playing the hand Providence has dealt me –
to shine a light into the tyrant's hollow soul.
May God protect me in the dangerous game I play.
Oh! –

PHILIP *appears before him.*] *

PHILIP.
What do you know of my son?

RODRIGO.
I used to know him well.
A fine young man – noble and upright –
I've never heard anyone speak ill of him –

PHILIP.
I have – I'm told he's eager to steal my crown. That he's
plotting with . . .

RODRIGO.
With whom?

PHILIP.
My wife.

RODRIGO.
Don't tell me you believe it? – Who dares say so?

PHILIP.
Common gossip says so. My courtiers say so. I must say so –
They have brought me evidence. Though . . .
My son is writing her letters . . . full of love. But – you're
right –
in my heart of hearts, I cannot believe – cannot *make* myself
believe –
my wife is not the best – the most honourable of ladies.
I do know the Duke of Alba hates my son.
I know my confessor fears the Queen.

* The bracketed speeches were omitted from the Sheffield Crucible production.

I know the Princess Eboli to be . . .
unfaithful to her mistress – jealous and proud.
Elizabeth's worth more than all of them – she must be
or I'll never trust my own judgement in anything . . . Then
I am lost.
Marquis, you've knelt at my feet and asked nothing.
I've never known that in a man.
Now I've something to ask of you.
Be my judge – judge them – judge me.
Befriend my son,
keep close watch on the Queen –
I'll see you have access to her –
But . . .
I must know the truth – only truth can heal me – the truth . . .
O give me back my peace of mind!

He turns upstage. RODRIGO *goes to him.*

Scene Twelve

QUEEN ELIZABETH'*s audience chamber. The* PAGE *places
a large jewel box on the table. The* DUCHESS OF OLIVAREZ
looks concerned. PRINCESS EBOLI *looks sick, mad, and very
nervous.*

ELIZABETH.
  Somebody must know what's happened to the key.
  Never mind, then – we'll have to break it open.

  Princess Eboli, are you still unwell? (*Not seriously concerned.*)
  Perhaps you're out of bed too soon –
  She looks so pale.

OLIVAREZ (*a hint of malice*).
  No, she's been too long on her back.
  The best cure for her sickness
  is to be up and doing.

ELIZABETH.
  I'm sorry I couldn't visit you.

OLIVAREZ.

    Custom does not allow the Queen of Spain
    to enter the chambers of the sick.
    But we hear the Princess Eboli was well provided for.

ELIZABETH.

    Go on. Break it open.

    The PAGE *does so. Diamonds and other jewellery spill out.*

EBOLI.

    Majesty, I beg permission to retire.

ELIZABETH.

    Of course –

EBOLI.

    I need to . . . Some air – I – (*Hurries out.*)

ELIZABETH.

    Hurry! – after her.

    Exit PAGE.

    The Princess has deceived us.
    Clearly she's still unwell – she should have stayed in her
    apartments –
    But . . . where . . . ?

    ELIZABETH *searches and discovers that letters and the
    portrait of* CARLOS *are missing from the cabinet. The*
    PAGE, *who has followed* EBOLI, *returns with a letter and
    hands it to* OLIVAREZ.

OLIVAREZ.

    Majesty,
    The Marquis of Posa – is here from the King.

ELIZABETH (*puzzled*).

    From the King? Surely you're mistaken.

    The PAGE *ushers* RODRIGO *in.*

    Marquis.

RODRIGO.

    Majesty.
    The King's message is for you alone.

OLIVAREZ *withdraws.*

ELIZABETH.
From the King?

RODRIGO.
It surprises you?

ELIZABETH.
Yes – it does.
What have you to do with the King?
Is this some double game? I abhor dishonesty –

RODRIGO.
I hate it, too.
Majesty, fate has placed me in the King's service
and I mean to serve him more faithfully –
more honourably than he could guess.

ELIZABETH.
Your errand?

RODRIGO.
The King's message –
his request – is that, for the present,
you grant no audience to the French Ambassador.

ELIZABETH.
Is that all?

RODRIGO.
All from His Majesty – yes.
From myself –

ELIZABETH.
No, no –
More than the King permits, I have no desire to hear –

RODRIGO.
There are some about you who wish you harm –
I would warn you to be vigilant,
but I know your innocence will shield you from all slanders –

ELIZABETH.
I'll ask again. Why are you here?

RODRIGO.
  The Prince –

ELIZABETH (*fast and low*).
  I thought as much: Carlos wishes to see me.
  I know – it needs no messenger.
  Tell me, Marquis, what good would it do either of us?
  Would it make Carlos happier –
  to know how close I am to despair ?

RODRIGO.
  It might give him strength – resolution.

ELIZABETH.
  For what?

RODRIGO.
  For what lies ahead of him.
  The Duke of Alba is named Viceroy of the Netherlands.
  His army will march within the week.

ELIZABETH (*almost to herself*).
  Merciful God!

RODRIGO.
  Only Carlos can prevent the bloodshed that must follow –
  Only to you, my lady, dare I reveal our enterprise,
  for only at your command would Carlos act upon it.

ELIZABETH.
  No – go no further!
  You'd have him betray his father –

RODRIGO.
  I'd have him rescue Flanders!

  ELIZABETH *is uneasy. She comes down and checks that
  nobody is listening.*

  He must leave Madrid, swiftly, secretly – steal a march on
  Alba –
  In Flanders his people will receive him with open arms –
  Think of it! Their young Prince comes among them –
  their King's beloved son – a saviour – a new beginning –
  The news will blaze through the Netherlands like a fire –

consuming all thought of war!
And when the King is told of Carlos' bloodless victory,
he will be forced to accept, and ratify, in Brussels the
Viceregency he refused him in Madrid.

ELIZABETH.
You'd place him in such danger? Carlos is young –

RODRIGO.
William of Orange is old and wise,
Egmont too – both were loyal servants to Charles the Fifth –
they're waiting to offer their service to his grandson.

ELIZABETH.
You terrify me, Marquis . . .
But of what consequence are my fears? – I see he must go.
For too long we've both been idle – clinging to past dreams –
Now he must act – I can no longer bear to watch him waste
away.

And I can promise him the support
of France, and Savoy.

RODRIGO.
He must hear it from your own mouth.
When can he see you – *how* can he see you?
You are both spied upon.

ELIZABETH.
There's worse – letters he wrote to me
have been stolen from this jewel box.
But, I'll find a way.
Say that I will see him.

Scene Thirteen

A choir. CARLOS, *waiting in the chapel for* RODRIGO, *is
reading letters. He is approached by* LERMA. *He replaces the
letters in a blue portfolio.*

LERMA.
Forgive me, Royal Highness – may I speak?

I hope you will believe me when I say
you have, in me, a friend at Court.

CARLOS.

Go on.

LERMA.

Do you know the Marquis of Posa?

CARLOS.

I do. An honourable man.

LERMA.

I've always thought so, Highness.
This morning he was summoned by the King . . .
They spent an hour together – most secretly.
When the Marquis left,
His Majesty gave order that for the future
he should be admitted, unannounced,
whenever he wished. I fear . . .

CARLOS.

What do you fear?

LERMA.

It's unprecedented – in all my years of service.
My fears are . . . well . . .
The King's favour can be a great corrupter of honesty.

CARLOS.

It won't corrupt the Marquis.

LERMA.

I hope you're right, Highness.
And how may one place a true value upon a man's honour
except by putting it to the test?

CARLOS.

If the Marquis is the man I take him for,
he will be tested and found true.

LERMA.

Then, at least you'll know you have one friend you can
trust.

CARLOS.

I find I will have two, Count Lerma.

CARLOS *gives him his hand to kiss.* LERMA *does so and withdraws.* CARLOS *takes the small blue portfolio and from it a bundle of letters which he begins to read. He is soon absorbed.* RODRIGO *comes silently to* CARLOS *who drops the letters.* RODRIGO *picks them up and hands them back to him.*

RODRIGO.

What are they?

CARLOS.

Old letters – a few from the Queen.
I hear you've been with my father?

RODRIGO.

Yes. I was summoned.

Slight pause.

CARLOS.

Go on.

RODRIGO.

Carlos, I've spoken to Elizabeth – she will see you –

CARLOS.

My father! What have you been saying to my father?
Why did he summon you?

RODRIGO.

I've no idea.
I can only suppose some well-meaning friend –

CARLOS.

He must have wanted something from you –

RODRIGO.

If –

CARLOS.

Or offered you something?

RODRIGO.

He offered me employment –

CARLOS.
But you refused him?

RODRIGO.
Of course I did –

CARLOS.
Did you part on good terms?

RODRIGO.
I –

CARLOS.
You said nothing about me?

RODRIGO.
Of course we spoke of you! – he's your father –

CARLOS.
We mustn't be seen together. (*Starts to leave.*)

RODRIGO.
But there's nobody here – Carlos – come back! –

CARLOS.
An hour with His Majesty –
and already you've acquired his tone of command –

RODRIGO.
Carlos! What's wrong with you?

CARLOS.
Nothing's wrong with me! You say you've spoken to the
Queen?

RODRIGO.
I have –

CARLOS.
What about?

RODRIGO.
I'm not sure you're in the right frame of mind
to hear what I have to say.

CARLOS.
Forgive me, Rodrigo.

I would not offend you for the world.
I'm desolate . . . desolate.

RODRIGO.

Elizabeth will see you –
how and where she cannot yet reveal,
but she has words to say to you – full of hope.
I think I see an end to this unhappiness.
Now give me those letters.

CARLOS.

My letters? Why?

RODRIGO.

And any notes, trifles –
anything that might be misinterpreted.
They must not fall into the wrong hands.

CARLOS.

Why should they? Why now?

RODRIGO.

They're safer with me – I won't be searched –
I shouldn't think there's any danger
but we must make sure.
Quickly.

CARLOS (*taking out the letters. Emptying his pockets of other
things*).

You'll keep them hidden?

RODRIGO.

Anything else?

CARLOS.

Rodrigo.
I've given into your trust –

RODRIGO.

Everything – I know.
Your life, your heart, could not be in safer keeping.
Farewell – farewell –

CARLOS.

No – don't go.
Give them back – there's something . . .

RODRIGO *hands them back.* CARLOS *extracts a letter and hands back the rest.*

You can't take this one.

RODRIGO.
Why? What is it?

CARLOS.
The letter she wrote secretly to me in Aranjuez – when I was at my lowest.
The letter you brought to me. Her words are my future. It's been my hope – my preserver.
I keep it always next to my heart.
And without it . . .

RODRIGO.
Carlos.

CARLOS.
I cannot part with it.

RODRIGO.
You know, that, above all, is the letter I must have.

CARLOS *hands it over.*

CARLOS.
Then . . .

He's about to go. Then he embraces RODRIGO *and looks searchingly into his eyes. He weeps.*

This is not my father's doing.
If I can be sure of anything
I'm sure of you.
Rodrigo.

He presses his face to RODRIGO*'s breast for a moment. Then goes quickly.*

RODRIGO.
Poor, loving, noble soul! –
I must torment you a while longer –
demanding your trust while arousing your deep suspicion.
Sleep out the night's storm, Carlos –
and I will awaken you in the bright tomorrow.

Scene Fourteen

KING PHILIP*'s study.* PHILIP *is sitting in an armchair, weak from lack of sleep and worry. He is looking at a new portrait of Clara Eugenia, his three-year-old daughter. He holds the miniature of* CARLOS *pressed to his heart.*

PHILIP.
  My daughter!
  Sweet, sweet, blessed childhood –
  joys I've never known.
  Her eyes, her every feature a miniature of mine –
  Do you love me, child?
  My daughter.
  Is this a father's love drawing me to my own.
  My son. (*Looking at the miniature of* CARLOS.
  Realisation.)

  It's his face – his I see in yours!
  I'm falling into madness – madness –

He lets the miniature fall. Enter LERMA, *in haste.*

LERMA.
  Majesty, the Queen –

PHILIP.
  No – I won't see her! Not now – Custom forbids –

She rushes in.

ELIZABETH.
  Majesty –
  Justice – '

PHILIP.
  I –

She kneels. PHILIP *is covered in confusion.*

ELIZABETH.
  Give me justice, Husband.
  Things have been stolen from –

PHILIP.
  What things?

ELIZABETH.
Things of value to me alone –

PHILIP.
Get up – Madame –

ELIZABETH.
Forgive me, sir – I will not
until I have your word,
you'll see the thief unmasked –

PHILIP.
Yet, Madame, stand –
How may I . . . Do stand.

She does.

ELIZABETH.
The thief's a man of rank – that's certain.
My casket contained diamonds – pearls –
jewels set in gold – all of great worth –
yet he stole only papers.

PHILIP.
Papers?

ELIZABETH.
Letters – from Don Carlos –

PHILIP (*astonished*).
Madame! –

ELIZABETH.
Our son.

PHILIP.
Letters from the Prince?

ELIZABETH.
Yes –

PHILIP.
You confess it to my face?

ELIZABETH.
Confess? What should I need to confess?

They are the letters – beautiful, loving letters – he wrote to
me at St Germain –
when we were first betrothed – letters handed to me by my
father . . .

PHILIP *freezes.*

Husband?
His picture – a miniature – that was taken, too.

Sees PHILIP*'s distress.*

What is it? – Majesty? What's wrong with you?

Sees the miniature and picks it up. After a pause:

Permit me one question –

PHILIP.
No – let me ask you –

ELIZABETH.
Was the thief acting upon your orders?

No reply.

I'll ask again – did you order this?
Did you?

PHILIP.
I did.

ELIZABETH.
Then, I forgive him, whoever he may be.
His shame is your own.

PHILIP.
Do you hold my honour in such contempt?

ELIZABETH.
Your honour!
O I tremble for it, sir!
My father was a king.
Do you think it honourable to treat your wife – a daughter
of the House of Valois – like a delinquent?
Do you set your traps for me?
It is my custom always to speak truthfully.
To hear the truth you have only to ask it kindly.

PHILIP.

Brave words, Madame –
You have a proud spirit –
What's between you?

ELIZABETH.

Between whom?

PHILIP.

Yourself and Don Carlos –

ELIZABETH.

What reason have I to lie?
I love him dearly, honourably,
as a mother should love any of her husband's children –

PHILIP.

Cunning and false –

ELIZABETH.

The truth!
I love your son as you should love him.
I would not fail him as a mother as you have failed him as a
father.

PHILIP.

I – fail – ! –

ELIZABETH.

He merits kinder treatment at your hands –

PHILIP.

Does he!

ELIZABETH.

He does.
Let me remind you, sir,
you once found sufficient worth in your son
to propose him as my husband –
the Prince of Spain for the Princess of France –
the world approved the match.
And you must teach me – for it's never been explained –
why he, whom I was required to hold most dear, must be a
stranger now.
I will be faithful to you, sir,

but I will not love at your requiring – nor hate neither.
You asked for truth.
You have it!

PHILIP.

Don't think a husband's love will make me weak –
You'll drive me to madness – madness! –

ELIZABETH.

If I've offended, what's my offence?

PHILIP.

Elizabeth! –

ELIZABETH.

If I've neglected some moth-eaten rule of courtesy, then tell me.
But, should the Queen wish to speak to the Prince,
She shall feel as free to do so in Spain
as she would in France.

PHILIP.

O these are dangerous waters, Madame!
Are you not afraid to look at me!

ELIZABETH.

Unhappy man! –

PHILIP.

I hardly know myself! – I'm grown unnatural! –
What comfort's kingship to me now?
What balm's in honour – faith! –

ELIZABETH (*sincerely*).

I pity you.

PHILIP.

Pity yourself – adulteress!

He knocks over the portrait of Clara Eugenia. In trying to prevent him destroying it, ELIZABETH *is knocked down too.* ELIZABETH *speaks with great dignity.*

ELIZABETH.

While I live, you'll not abuse another child.
I'll take our daughter and go home – to France –

PHILIP (*embarrassed*).
  Elizabeth!

ELIZABETH.
  O – I can't – Help me –

She reaches the door and swoons, hitting her head.

PHILIP.
  Dear God! What's happening!

Concerned, he rushes to catch her but too late.

  It wasn't my fault – Blood? – Get up!
  Elizabeth, you mustn't shame me – Lerma! Stand up!
  Stand – people will come in – they mustn't see –
  The Court will say I –
  O stand up – must I beg you? –
  Elizabeth!

She pulls herself up, helped by PHILIP. *He holds onto her.*

  Lerma! Lerma!

LERMA *comes in with* OLIVAREZ *followed by* ALBA *and*
DOMINGO, *and the* PAGE.

  The Queen's unwell – help her to her apartments – Duchess –

LERMA *and* OLIVAREZ *help her out, as* RODRIGO
enters. Sounds of distress as they go. To ALBA *and*
DOMINGO:

  O my councillors – corrupters of my mind – my reason! –
  Are you proud of your malevolence?

DOMINGO.
  Majesty!

ALBA.
  How are we to blame?

PHILIP.
  For raising doubts in me where there were none!
  For choking me with truth and falsehood mixed –
  for stealing away my sanity –

ALBA.
You asked us what we knew –

PHILIP.
May Hell reward you for what you've known.
And Heaven forgive me for the wrong I've done her.
She's pure – she's innocent!

He stumbles. ALBA *rushes to help him.* PHILIP *rejects his help.*

Marquis –

RODRIGO *helps him up.* PHILIP *makes a great effort to compose himself. He waves away* DOMINGO *and* ALBA *who exchange amazed glances.*

Away! Go! You were not summoned –
I have no need of you.

RODRIGO *puts a pile of* CARLOS' *letters on the desk.*

More letters –

RODRIGO.
I took these papers from your son's letter-case.
You must examine them.

PHILIP.
Is he . . . Am I betrayed? (*He begins to read the letters.*)

Letters to Carlos from the Emperor, my father – What?
Full of affection – I never knew –
These drawings – a castle? – a child's letters addressed to
me . . . and never sent.
Some lines from Tacitus' *Germania:*
'urgentibus imperii fatis' – (*Roughly: fate drives on our empire.*)
and this? – the writing's familiar . . .

'This key unlocks . . . The Queen's apartments . . . '
Who has . . . ? – 'Free to confess our love . . . '

He seems to collapse into guilty realisation, tinged with relief.

I know the hand.

RODRIGO.

It's not the Queen's writing.

PHILIP.

No . . . The Princess Eboli.

RODRIGO.

Yes, it is Eboli's. I questioned Her Majesty's page.
Innocently, he took your son the letter and the key,
at the Princess's request.

Pause.

PHILIP.

Like an angel you've watched over your king –
An angel sent by Heaven!

The rest are devils! – Alba – Domingo –
It was Princess Eboli who stole from the Queen –
poisoning my mind with fictions of my wife's
unfaithfulness –
She who is herself most faithless.
How many others are conspiring against me?
O I am every man's fool!

RODRIGO.

Be thankful there's no harm done –

PHILIP.

O Marquis, Marquis, there is, there is!
I've shamed my wife – perhaps I've lost my son –

Enter LERMA. RODRIGO *hastily collects* CARLOS'
letters and replaces them in his breast pocket.

Lerma, is she recovered?

LERMA.

Still weak, Majesty. But calmer now.

PHILIP.

Say I will come to her.

LERMA *bows, looks suspiciously at* RODRIGO, *and exits.*

RODRIGO.

The Queen is loved by everyone.
When the Prince learns what's happened here –

PHILIP.

You must be watchful, Marquis – now more than ever
My son's reckless, headstrong, ambitious –
He begged to lead my armies into Flanders – but now
perhaps . . .
Am I driving him into the arms of my enemies?

RODRIGO.

He'd be a prize among the rebels.
And if he tried to flee to them –

PHILIP.

What have I done, what have I done?
If I've turned him against me –

RODRIGO.

I shall be vigilant.

PHILIP.

I commit him to your care.

RODRIGO.

Then . . .
Give me some authority . . .

Pause.

Should he try to leave Madrid
it might be necessary to restrain him.

PHILIP *takes the ring from his finger and places it on*
RODRIGO*'s.*

PHILIP.

Take this ring.
Borrow my supremacy.
In these few hours you have been more to me
than all those old, old men – their lifetimes of loyal service . . .
Nor will I hide my favour from the world.
I choose you as my friend.
Wear my majesty upon your brow – command, control, be
envied – be feared.
Go, now. Go –
Bring me sleep for my nights and healing for my soul.

Scene Fifteen

Rushing towards QUEEN ELIZABETH*'s apartments:*
CARLOS *in great turmoil.* LERMA *comes from* ELIZABETH.

CARLOS.
Lerma! Is it true? Quickly –

LERMA.
Is what true, Highness?

CARLOS.
My father attacked the Queen – she was carried bleeding
from his chamber –

LERMA.
No – no.

CARLOS.
No juggling, man! Upon your honour?

LERMA.
Her Majesty fainted.
She fell and cut herself –

CARLOS.
You swear it?

LERMA.
That's all –

CARLOS.
She's in no danger?

LERMA.
She is not . . .
(*He lowers his voice.*) But for yourself – a word.
The Marquis of Posa has shown letters of yours to His
Majesty –

The shock registers.

CARLOS.
I don't believe you. You're lying to me!

LERMA *bows and turns away.*

How has he offended you
that you seek to make me doubt him?

LERMA.

Highness, I regret the pain it causes you
but I saw what I saw –

CARLOS.

I won't listen! –

LERMA.

The Duke of Alba is disgraced,
And the King's authority given to the Marquis.

CARLOS.

O – God in Heaven!
I gave him her letter – it's in his power to ruin her and
destroy me!
What is he doing? – What purpose can it serve?

LERMA.

Royal Highness –

CARLOS (*very agitated, banging on the doors*).

I must warn the Queen –

LERMA.

No, sir –

CARLOS.

At once!

EBOLI *comes from* ELIZABETH's *apartments.*

Princess – help me! –
You must help –

EBOLI.

Carlos –

LERMA.

Sir –

CARLOS.

I must see her – speak to her! –
Listen to me – I'll explain everything –

EBOLI.
No – in the name of God –

CARLOS.
Take me to her!

He tries to force his way into ELIZABETH's *apartment.
As* RODRIGO *arrives with a young officer –* COUNT
CORDUA *– the doors are shut in* CARLOS' *face.*

RODRIGO.
Carlos!

CARLOS.
I must see her –

RODRIGO (*harshly, to* EBOLI).
What has he said to you?
Believe nothing – say nothing –

A few other COURTIERS *arrive.*

CARLOS.
God help me! –

LERMA *hurries the onlookers away.*

RODRIGO.
The Prince is sick –
a fever – doesn't know what he's saying – can't you see? –

CARLOS (*to* EBOLI).
Our lives depend upon it! –
I beg you, open these doors!

RODRIGO.
Carlos – you must control yourself –
No – no more –

CARLOS *attacks* RODRIGO *who holds him, placing his
hand over his mouth.* CARLOS *collapses.*

Count Cordua, in the name of the King –
The Prince is your prisoner.

EBOLI *gasps and tries to run.*

Hold her!

A SOLDIER *does so.*

Royal Highness, for your own safety you must surrender
your sword.

As CARLOS *is in a state of collapse,* RODRIGO *takes it.*

Count, as you will answer to the King,
I charge you let His Highness speak to nobody.
I will come to you, Prince, within the hour.

CARLOS *is taken away, only half comprehending what is
happening to him. As he comes to his senses he looks back,
bewildered, at* RODRIGO, *who turns away from him.*

CARLOS.
Rodrigo!

EBOLI *tries to retreat into* ELIZABETH's *apartments.*
RODRIGO *grabs her. He is still holding* CARLOS' *sword.*

RODRIGO.
This is your doing!

EBOLI.
What have I done?
I'm innocent of every –

RODRIGO.
What has he said to you?

EBOLI.
By what authority do you threaten me?
What have I done!

RODRIGO.
It's what you will do.
Have you more poison for the King's ears?
More lies? A queen's virtue –
A prince's honour – what have you left to slander?
I should –

EBOLI.
Kill me – finish me –
I don't want to live –
Do it! Do it! Why do you hesitate?

She tries to hold the point of CARLOS' *sword to her throat.*
RODRIGO *pushes her away, beats on the door with the hilt*
of the sword and runs off. Then the DUCHESS OF
OLIVAREZ *appears and kneels to help* EBOLI. *Then the*
PAGE. *Finally,* QUEEN ELIZABETH.

EBOLI.
Help – help me – They're taking him to prison.

OLIVAREZ.
Who?

EBOLI.
The Marquis Posa has arrested him,
by order of the King.

OLIVAREZ.
Who's arrested?

EBOLI.
The Prince – Carlos –

OLIVAREZ.
You're mistaken. It can't be true.

ELIZABETH.
The Marquis took him?

EBOLI.
Yes, Your Majesty.

ELIZABETH (*to herself*).
But why?

EBOLI.
He's going to his death!

OLIVAREZ.
You can't know what you're saying – he's the King's son –

EBOLI (*shaken by sobs*).
But I've murdered him.

ELIZABETH.
What are you thinking? Why should Carlos die?

EBOLI.
I am to blame – I confess – confess –

ELIZABETH (*firmly*).
>Princess – calm yourself.
>You must tell me what you know.
>If Carlos is in danger –

She takes hold of EBOLI.

EBOLI.
>No, no, no –

ELIZABETH.
>What can you confess?

EBOLI.
>A saint looks harshly upon me –
>An angel of light! O how have I offended you!
>I'm the devil – I stole your letters –

ELIZABETH.
>But why? How could you do such a thing?

EBOLI.
>They forced me –

ELIZABETH.
>Who –

EBOLI.
>I took them to the King –

ELIZABETH.
>But why?

EBOLI.
>Pride! – revenge on them – all of them!
>I loved where I was not loved – the Prince. Carlos . . .

ELIZABETH.
>You did these things for love?
>Come – Stand up, Princess. You're forgiven –
>No – I forgive you everything –

EBOLI (*in a whisper*).
>There's worse –
>I'm your husband's whore –
>O –

The women gasp. EBOLI presses her face to the floor,
shaking. ELIZABETH goes quickly into her apartment
followed by her LADIES, except OLIVAREZ. The PAGE
closes the doors behind them.

What's to become of me?

OLIVAREZ.

You must give me your cross and your keys.

EBOLI makes no move. OLIVAREZ raises her to her knees,
and removes the cross of her order from EBOLI's bosom.
Then she takes the keys that hang upon a jewel at her waist.

EBOLI.

Is it not permitted that I kiss her hand? –
For the last time?

OLIVAREZ.

It is not the custom for a disgraced . . .

She breaks off in tears.

You must go to the Convent of the Blessed Virgin.
There, you'll be told what's been decided.

EBOLI.

Will I never see her again?

OLIVAREZ embraces her, without looking at her face, then
goes into the apartment. EBOLI follows but OLIVAREZ
gently closes the doors against her. EBOLI goes in great
distress. Alarm bells tolling. Sounds of confusion. GUARDS
marching. CARLOS is taken to prison. Shots. Cannon fire.
A mob heard in the distance.

Scene Sixteen

Darkness. Later that night. A few candles burning. ELIZABETH
alone in her chamber, very agitated, pacing up and down.

PAGE.

Madame, the Marquis Posa is here.
He comes on the King's authority.

ELIZABETH.
Admit him.

RODRIGO *comes in, pale and sombre.*

Why? They're saying you've arrested Carlos.

RODRIGO.
I have. So now he's safe.

ELIZABETH.
Safe? You're playing a dangerous game.

RODRIGO.
A game I've already lost.

ELIZABETH (*frustration*).
Riddles!

RODRIGO.
I'm lost. But Carlos is safe.
My life's of little consequence –

ELIZABETH.
Your life!

RODRIGO.
It will buy him time.
Now listen – listen to me.
Carlos must leave Madrid tonight – leave Spain –

ELIZABETH.
Tonight!

RODRIGO.
His horses are waiting at St Lawrence' Church.
Give him this money – more if you have it –
and these – (*A package of papers.*)
There were so many things I had to say to him –
of great urgency and importance . . .
Others of small consequence except to the two of us.
Now, there's so little time left.
The words I leave unsaid you must speak for me.

ELIZABETH.
Do you mean to terrify me, sir? Where are you going?

RODRIGO.
> May I tell you
> the most important thing of all?

> *Slight pause.*

> I have had the good fortune –
> not knowing why I should deserve it –
> to love the son of a king.
> I've devoted my life to him –
> and in him I saw the vision of a better world.
> Hope grew with our friendship – until that vision became
> real –
> and now it's attainable, substantial – within our grasp.
> Do you understand what I've been doing, Madame?
> I have planted in Carlos' soul an earthly paradise –
> safe haven for a million other souls.
> Together we have charted a course for a future full of promise.
> He'll lead his people into this bright new world . . .
> but I can go no further at his side.

> This farewell sacrifice of love I've hidden in your heart,
> knowing he'll find it there – (*He turns away.*)

ELIZABETH.
> A sacrifice? Of love?

RODRIGO.
> I've kept my oath.
> Now he must keep his –

> And here's the beauty of it – the King will open his heart to
> his son –
> That heart may seem frozen but it will thaw. It remains a
> good heart.
> He'll be a guide to Carlos, a support – a father!
> My sacrifice will bring father and son together.

> For it will mean the end of Alba –
> all the Albas, the Domingos, the rule of ceremony,
> the secrecy, the corruption in the Court – all will be swept
> away.
> I've broken the hold they had on the King.
> But Carlos must learn kingship

and accomplish alone what we planned together.
Keep him true, Madame, keep him true –

ELIZABETH.

Unhappy man – what have you done? –

RODRIGO.

Inspire him, never abandon him,
love him unchangingly –
Will you promise, Madame?
Do I have your promise?
You must admit your love for Carlos.
It will give him such strength –

ELIZABETH.

I shall obey my heart – I promise you that.

RODRIGO.

And now –

He kisses her hand and starts to go.

ELIZABETH.

Is there no more I can do for you?

RODRIGO.

No more than you've promised.

ELIZABETH.

I have the courage.

RODRIGO.

I'm sure of it.

ELIZABETH.

Is there no help?

RODRIGO.

None. (*He turns to her.*)
O God – the beauty of the world –
Life is so beautiful.
But what is a life?

He goes quickly.

Scene Seventeen

Outside KING PHILIP*'s inner sanctum.* ALBA *and*
DOMINGO *wait nervously.* LERMA *comes out of* PHILIP*'s
room.*

LERMA.
He's asking for the Marquis.

ALBA.
The Marquis has disappeared. Everybody's looking for him.

Enter COUNT CORDUA.

CORDUA.
Count Lerma, I must see His Majesty.

LERMA.
He's seeing nobody.

CORDUA.
He'll see me –
It's most urgent – a matter of State importance.
Take him these –

Gives letters, exit LERMA.

ALBA.
You're in for a long wait.

CORDUA.
Oh?

ALBA.
You should have addressed yourself to the Marquis of Posa,
who imprisons princes, and captivates kings.

CORDUA.
And is in the pay of our enemies in Flanders.

DOMINGO.
What! What did you say?

ALBA.
Oh –

CORDUA.
 I have intercepted a communication –
 it's addressed to the Prince of Nassau and Orange –

ALBA.
 William of Orange!

DOMINGO.
 This is treason!

CORDUA.
 It would seem so.

DOMINGO.
 You've done well, sir.

CORDUA.
 I've done my duty, sir.

 LERMA *comes out.*

LERMA.
 Come.

 CORDUA *is let into* PHILIP*'s room.*

 No sign of Posa?

DOMINGO.
 They're still looking.

LERMA.
 Say nothing of this. (*Goes back in.*)

DOMINGO.
 Note that. Posa – not 'The Marquis'

ALBA.
 What's going on?
 The Prince in prison – not even the King knows why –

DOMINGO.
 And the royal favourite doesn't condescend
 to come and offer explanations.

ALBA.
 I'm going to listen at the door. (*He does.*)

DOMINGO.

What are they saying?

ALBA.

Be quiet!

DOMINGO.

We should be in there.

ALBA.

Shhh. He'll call us when we're needed.

DOMINGO.

We're not needed.

Our days of glory are gone.

ALBA.

They are, they are . . .

You see the ruin of a once proud man.

He comes from the door. DOMINGO *takes his place.*

I was his right arm – the man for whom all doors flew open.

DOMINGO.

They've stopped talking.

I can't hear –

He springs away from the door.

Enter the PRINCE OF PARMA, *the* DUKE OF MEDINA
SIDONIA, *and other* GRANDEES.

PARMA.

I must speak to my uncle.

ALBA.

His Majesty is receiving no one.

PARMA.

Who's in there? –

MEDINA SIDONIA.

Is the Marquis with him?

ALBA.

The Marquis chooses to absent himself.

DOMINGO.
Everybody's looking for him –

PARMA.
We came as soon as we heard.
The people have surrounded the palace – they're demanding
to see Carlos –

MEDINA SIDONIA.
Is it true?

DOMINGO.
Is what true?

PARMA.
The Prince, my cousin, has been arrested –

MEDINA SIDONIA.
By the Marquis Posa?

DOMINGO.
Yes, it's true.

PARMA.
Why? On what charge?

ALBA.
Ask the Marquis.

DOMINGO.
We're told nothing.

PARMA.
It's high treason to arrest a Prince of the Blood,
without the authority of Parliament signed and sealed by the
King.
I know of no precedent –

ALBA.
I'm sure you're right, Prince –

MEDINA SIDONIA.
Is there some conspiracy?

PARMA.
If so, it must be stopped –

A cry of despair, from PHILIP's *room.*

I must go to my uncle –

ALBA.

I'll come with you –

He rushes to the door – as he does so, it is thrown open by the GUARD. LERMA *hurries out.*

LERMA.

He'll see the Duke of Alba. Nobody else.

ALBA *enters.*

When Posa arrives, you're to keep him here.

DOMINGO.

You're pale as death, sir.
May we know what's happening?

LERMA.

The devil's work.

DOMINGO.

The devil?

PARMA.

What is?

LERMA.

The King is weeping.

PARMA.

The King doesn't weep. He never has.

LERMA.

The King is weeping.

A bell. LERMA *rushes back into the room.*

Scene Eighteen

Night. Prison. A door with a grill. RODRIGO *appears and is let in. He sits opposite* CARLOS *and looks at him silently and sadly for a few moments.*

CARLOS.

I knew you wouldn't abandon me, Rodrigo.

RODRIGO.
  Did you doubt me?

CARLOS.
  O yes. But only for a moment.
  Now I understand everything – I've been working it out.

RODRIGO.
  Have you?

CARLOS.
  I failed, didn't I?
  Our great work – 'When I am King of Spain,' remember?
  But I failed you, I've failed my people.
  Now you're going to finish it alone.
  You saw I was not equal to the task.
  I'm weak – flawed –
  This fatal, all-absorbing love of mine
  betrayed us both – endangered our enterprise.

RODRIGO.
  Is that what you thought?

CARLOS.
  So you took my letter and gave it to my father –
  selling the worthless affection of a prince
  to buy the favour and the trust of a king.
  There was no other way.

RODRIGO.
  I was tempted – I confess it.
  All that power, to a man unused to wielding it, is very
  seductive.
  There was a moment when I thought I might accomplish on
  my own
  the task you faltered in.

CARLOS.
  Now you'll be his good angel – his guiding light.
  You'll use his own authority to lead our people to a better
  future.
  Rodrigo, if I'm to die for your vision – for our vision –
  I'll die willingly.

> But did you have to bring her down?
> Could you not have saved Elizabeth?
> That letter ruins her as well as me.

RODRIGO (*passing it to him*).
> This letter?
> Take it – it's safer with you now.
> You're going to Flanders.

CARLOS.
> But . . . ? You didn't show it to the King?

RODRIGO.
> Of course not – not that one.
> The letters I showed him proved your innocence.

CARLOS.
> He doesn't know I love Elizabeth?

RODRIGO.
> He knows nothing ill of you.

CARLOS.
> Then why am I imprisoned?

RODRIGO.
> For your own safety.
> Like the boy you are, you'd have shouted love and defiance
> from the rooftops –
> They'd have heard it in Madrid,
> applauded it in Paris – and punished it in Rome.
>
> You'd have confessed everything to the Princess Eboli –
> confirmed her suspicions –
> All that I had taken pains to conceal.
> Carlos, it was Eboli denounced you to the King –

CARLOS.
> O God what have I done! I see it all –

ALBA *enters with a* GUARD.

ALBA.
> Posa?
> So this is where you're hiding.

RODRIGO.
 This is where I am, Duke.

ALBA.
 You have something belonging to His Majesty?

 ALBA *holds out his hand.* RODRIGO *places* KING
 PHILIP's *ring in it.* ALBA *clenches his fist around it. Bows
 low to* CARLOS. CARLOS *looks at* RODRIGO, *horrified.*
 RODRIGO *looks on* ALBA *with contempt.*

 Royal Highness,
 My errand is to you.
 On His Majesty's express command,
 I have the honour to return your sword.
 You are free.

 He bows, offering the sword.

CARLOS.
 First I'm thrown into prison,
 then I'm released –
 But nobody has had the courtesy to tell me why.

ALBA.
 An error, Highness.
 His Majesty was misled.

CARLOS.
 I was arrested on my father's orders?

ALBA.
 Indirectly, Highness.

CARLOS.
 Then tell the King – directly –
 I will not accept my sword at the hands of the Duke of
 Alba.
 If my father is king, I am his kingdom's heir.
 If I have offended, let me answer to the Parliament.
 If there is no offence, tell the King – who has offended me –
 to fetch my sword here, and offer it himself.

ALBA (*shocked*).
 Highness, I will go with you to His Majesty –

CARLOS.

Sir, you will not.

I'm staying here.

Now go and deliver my message.

ALBA *bows out. The door is slammed behind him. The*
GUARDS *remain outside.*

RODRIGO.

Now thank God for all his mercies, Carlos.

It's working. This means you're free – and above suspicion!

CARLOS.

But you are not.

CARLOS *is in deadly shock as he begins to realise how*
RODRIGO *has incriminated himself to draw away*
PHILIP's *suspicion of him.*

RODRIGO.

I am, I am – for the first time in my life, I am free.

I can hold you to my heart, equal in love –

I've given everything for this moment.

Listen to me.

There was no other way –

I had to draw the King's suspicion upon myself.

My mistake was not to confide in you –

I thought you'd . . .

But now you're free to act.

And whatever they may tell you,

promise me you'll not give way to despair?

Carlos, you're going to lose me – a fool would say for ever.

But be a man – take all my strength –

you must complete the task we began so long ago.

CARLOS.

Rodrigo.

What have you done?

How have you drawn suspicion on yourself?

RODRIGO.

I wrote to Flanders – to William of Orange.

Letters full of plots and revolution –

incriminating myself but clearing you and the Queen –

CARLOS.
But all letters –

RODRIGO.
I told you I was no novice in these affairs!
By now the King must have them on his desk.
If Count Cordua has done his duty.

CARLOS.
We're lost! We're lost!

RODRIGO.
You are not!

CARLOS.
Thoughtless folly – poor innocent –
I've dragged you down with me!
Do you think my father will not revenge himself! –
Do you think he'll forgive this deception?

RODRIGO.
Deception? This deception is your escape –
Who's to tell my letters are fictions?

CARLOS.
Who's to tell? I'll tell him!
You think I'd risk your life? –

RODRIGO.
Are you mad! My life's over!
Let's not waste the time that's left to me –
I've so much to say to you –

CARLOS.
No, no – (*He hammers on the door.*)

RODRIGO.
Did I speak up for you? –
When we were boys, and you were flogged?

CARLOS.
O –

RODRIGO.
Listen. Carlos,
For Flanders' sake, for your people's freedom . . .

We each have one clear purpose in life.
To be King, and to rule well is yours.
To die – to make it possible – that's mine.

CARLOS.
No! No!
You will not die! – We'll go to him – arm in arm –
'Father,' I'll say, 'A friend has done all this
to save his friend!' Believe me, he'll forgive us –
he'll weep – he's my father! Yes – he's cold,
but he's not a monster!
How could he refuse me?
He'll applaud my action –

A shot is fired through the grill – it seems to have missed its target.

What . . . Who was that meant for?

RODRIGO (*still upright*).
I think it was meant for me. (*He sinks down.*)

CARLOS.
Rodrigo! (*He holds him in his arms.*)

RODRIGO.
He's wasted no time . . . your father.
Escape – you must escape. Nothing else matters.
Elizabeth – will tell you how. Carlos.
Do you hear what I say?
Get far away from here.
Your horses . . . there's a ship . . .
Carlos – (*Dies.*)

CARLOS.
I hear –

CARLOS lies as if dead next to the body. PHILIP enters followed by ALBA, DOMINGO, and all the other GRANDEES. He sees what appears to be two bodies and steps back, horrified. He approaches them and looks down in silence. CARLOS, dazed, sits upright. The GRANDEES form a semi-circle around him.

PHILIP.

O my son – Prince!
Receive your sword.
I have been betrayed – the fool and victim of evil men.

CARLOS sits up slowly.

Your rightful place is in your father's arms.
Come to me, my son, my son –

*He lifts CARLOS up and embraces him. Places the sword
in his hand. CARLOS accepts this, quite unconscious of
what is happening to him. For a long time it seems as if
father and son are united. Then CARLOS stares at his
father. Slowly places his hand on PHILIP's forehead.*

CARLOS.

Baptised in blood.
Blood upon your hands.
I can't embrace you, Father. (*Gently pushes him away.*)

PHILIP.

Come, my lords. Follow me. (*He turns to the door.*)

CARLOS (*shaking his sword from its scabbard*).

Stay where you are!

All the GRANDEES draw and protect PHILIP.

GRANDEES.

Treason! Treason!

*PHILIP presses down their swords and advances on
CARLOS.*

PHILIP.

Put up your swords.
This is my son.
Nature binds us.
He'll not shed the blood of the Lord's anointed.

CARLOS.

Nature!
What have you to do with nature?
Blood's your nature, butchery's your nature –

Look here! A man! God's creation! (*Over the body.*)
You make a slaughterhouse of nature! –

PHILIP (*mildly*).
How could you know he was your enemy?
I did this to save you from him.

CARLOS.
This man was no one's enemy.
He was my friend! My soul – half myself!

Shock among the GRANDEES.

He died to save my life!
Broken and bleeding – (*Goes back to* RODRIGO.)
My soul, my only life – forgive me – I have betrayed our sacred bond
to these grey, lifeless shadows.

(*To* PHILIP.) The honours you would have heaped upon him
he laid at my feet –
Your great authority
he wielded only for my safety.

ALBA.
He was a traitor –
We have his letters to the Prince of Orange –
We have the proof!

CARLOS.
Fictions! – to draw your bloodhounds from the scent –
to hide my purposes – I am the traitor!
Rebellion's bred in my blood and bones!
And now I swear – I'll save my people from your tyranny!
How could you – for all your intelligencing –
your secret codes, ciphers, and spies –
fall for such a gross deception?
(*To* PHILIP.) Did you think yourself worthy of his friendship?
Imagine you could woo him with your love and favour?

PHILIP *has been standing thunderstruck – staring at the ground. His terrified* GRANDEES *study him – hoping for some guidance.*

ALBA.

> Majesty – end this dreadful silence.
> What shall we do? Speak to us.

CARLOS.

> He could have given you everything –
> The peace of mind you crave – the love of your people –
> who knows? – perhaps even a measure of happiness.
> But look at him now.
> Now you have nobody.
> Nobody can help you.
> What is a life?

He suddenly jabs his sword towards PHILIP*'s throat. All the* GRANDEES *jump.* PHILIP *seems not to care. He raises his head and looks steadily at his son.* CARLOS *places his sword in* PHILIP*'s hand.*

> Take back my sword.
> Resume your tyranny – murder your child – be perfect in infamy!
> Go – Live among strangers.
> May your Empire grow and prosper!
> Where will you find a son to leave it to?
> Here lies my inheritance.

He sinks down next to the body and is oblivious to what goes on around him. The noise outside has been getting louder.

CORDUA (*off*).

> Where is the King?

PHILIP.

> Have you nothing to say, lords? What counsel can you give me?
> Eyes on the ground – all faces turn from me?
> Your silence is a judgement on your king.

CORDUA, *followed by the* QUEEN'S PAGE, *comes to the* DUKE OF ALBA.

CORDUA.

> Sir,
> The people of Madrid are up in arms.

They're saying Prince Carlos is in danger –
demanding to see him.

ALBA (*to the* GRANDEES).

We must protect His Majesty.
Sire, you must come away –
for your own safety –

PHILIP.

They're my people! Why are they asking for my son? Am *I*
not their king?
This Empire's mine – who would dispossess me? – who
would dare?
Am I not King, my lords? Are you all traitors – all of you!
Swear allegiance to the boy, then!
They whimper at his wailing,
whisper in huddles – rehearse their betrayals –
Go on!
Kneel to him – your stripling, springtime king.
I have grown old – too cold for rule and sway –
I'm no king – nothing –

ALBA.

Royal liege – our loyalty is to you alone –

The GRANDEES *affirm.*

PHILIP (*tearing off his gown*).

Here! Robe him in my majesty!
Seat him in my throne – set my crown upon his head –
give Charlemagne's imperial sceptre into his hand!
And trample me back into the dust I came from.
It's what my people want! Let it come – I welcome it!

He collapses into the arms of ALBA *and* DOMINGO *– the*
GRANDEES *gather round, making sounds of distress.*

ALBA.

Stand back there! – get him to his chamber –

LERMA.

Dear God in Heaven –

MEDINA SIDONIA.

Give him air –

LERMA.

Is he conscious?

PARMA.

Uncle –

Exeunt in confusion all but CARLOS. *The* PAGE *remains looking down at him. At first,* CARLOS *seems hardly aware of him.*

PAGE.

Highness! Royal Highness.

I have a message from the Queen. (*Shows a ring.*)

She must speak to you –

a matter of great urgency and importance.

CARLOS.

There's nothing urgent, nothing of importance in all this world –

PAGE.

She has much to tell you –

secrets entrusted to her by the Marquis Posa.

CARLOS.

Take me to her –

PAGE.

Sir – not yet! Be patient.

You must wait until nightfall – when the watch is changed.

Everywhere the guard has been doubled.

CARLOS.

Then how may I come to her?

PAGE.

There is a secret way into her chapel –

CARLOS.

But how –

PAGE.

I will show you how.

Meet me an hour before midnight

in the Long Gallery.

May I take her your answer?

CARLOS.

I'll not fail her.

LERMA *appears in the doorway.*

Leave me now.

The PAGE *exits.*

LERMA.

Royal Highness, you must save yourself.
I've never seen the King in such a rage – quite out of his senses –
Your life's in danger – you must leave at once. At once!

CARLOS.

I must see the Queen –

LERMA.

No, no! It's too dangerous –

CARLOS.

I'm in God's hands –

LERMA.

I trust so – but you must leave Madrid.
At once! There is not a moment to be lost.
Believe me – as you value your life.
The city's seething – the people up in arms –
the confusion will cover your escape.
Here, take these weapons.

Gives a box of pistols and a dagger.

I pray God you'll have no need of them.

CARLOS.

Good old man, thank you, thank you –

LERMA.

Go quickly, and God go with you –
And guide us all to better times.
My Prince, receive my homage.

He kneels and kisses CARLOS' *hand.*

CARLOS.
You'll move me to tears.

LERMA.
Our kingdom's hope! Return in glory.
My children will live to serve you
though I'll be long gone.
Rule Europe with compassion –
but take no revenge upon our royal master.
He forced the Emperor Charles, his father, from the throne –
he's punished for it now.
Let it not end in shedding blood of innocents.
Rule well, and may God give you strength.
Now, quickly – Go!

LERMA *exits in haste*. CARLOS *returns to* RODRIGO'*s body.*

Scene Nineteen

In KING PHILIP'*s audience chamber. The* GRANDEES *nervous.* PHILIP'*s appearance is wild and disordered – the days without sleep are telling.*

DOMINGO.
Speak to him.

ALBA.
He won't hear. Majesty –

PHILIP.
Don't come near me!
Down on your knees, you traitors!
I'll have submission! I want proof of your loyalty –
Kneel! – Grovel! On the ground – dust is your element!
I raised you from dust.
Do you think because I let one man come near to me
the rest of you are freed from your servility?

ALBA.

    Sire, think no more of Posa –

DOMINGO.

    A more subtle enemy opposes you now –

ALBA.

    Your son's the danger –

DOMINGO.

    Don Carlos has threatened your throne –
    The people will swear allegiance to him –

ALBA.

    Unless you act, Sire –
    Madrid will crown him –

PHILIP.

    Let them! Let them crown him!
    The people love him – all men love him – he had a friend
    who loved him – a friend who died for him . . .

    In all my years, in all my endless lands,
    I found only one free spirit – *one!* – one man of vision –
    and he gave his life for a boy . . . for my wretched,
    weakling son.
    I offered him Empires –
    I would have given him the future
    if only he had given me his love.

ALBA.

    Our King's quite lost to us. Out of his wits.
    Even in death this Marquis possesses him.

PHILIP (*sits on the ground. In a world of his own*).

    He was a soul . . . I could have loved.
    He could have been a son to me.
    He was life's new beginning –
    a bright new day – a cloudless sky –
    an end to past desolation – war – killing . . .
    Together we'd have been invincible – immortal.
    O who can bring back the dead to me?

    The GRANDEES *are horror-struck, embarrassed.*

DOMINGO.
  He's bewitched.

PARMA (*crossing himself*).
  Witchcraft?

DOMINGO.
  I see devils about him.

PARMA.
  God protect us!

ALBA.
  Royal Majesty –

PHILIP.
  Carlos!
  Philip, Carlos, Philip, Carlos . . .
  The father's feeling the chill wind of autumn –
  leaves yellowing, dry and old . . . Dying.

  GRANDEES *cross themselves.*

  The son will rise in glory – his day is dawning.
  Crossing yourselves?
  They're praying for my death – they can't wait for it –
  Can you!

  *During the next speech he regains his former power and
  stature, shaking off the tiredness, and weakness of the past
  scenes, and grows monstrous.*

  Well, I'm still here. Still here! I'll make them stoop.
  I'll grow young again to spite them all.
  Nature – raging – renews my strength –
  I feel my powers returning, my mind quickening!
  I'll set men laughing at this dead Posa –
  I'll mock his dreams into childish fantasies –

  Without me this age is unremarkable.
  Without me my people cannot thrive.
  Without me my Empire's so much dust . . .

  In the evening of my life
  I'll poison the land – burn all lands that will not submit –
  Flanders, Brabant, Holland, and the rest

I'll so blight their good earth –
that for ten – twenty generations after me
no field will yield a single fruitful ear.

My Marquis made humanity his idol.
Idolatry must be punished,
idols cast into the flames . . .

Where is the Prince?

DOMINGO.
    Gone.

ALBA.
    His horses are missing from the stables.
    I fear he's already on his way to Flanders.

DOMINGO.
    He'll make for Cadiz –

PHILIP.
    Are there lights in the Queen's apartments?

CORDUA.
    No, Sire.

LERMA.
    Her Majesty has dismissed her gentlewomen.
    The Duchess reports the Queen retired early.

PHILIP.
    I wonder, I wonder, I wonder –

A chill descends. Suddenly we are aware that the CARDINAL
GRAND INQUISITOR, *ninety years old, blind, leaning on
a stick and led by* DOMINICAN MONKS *has entered. As
he comes down,* LORDS *kneel, kiss the hem of his robe, and
depart. He blesses them. The* INQUISITOR, *his* GUIDES,
and KING PHILIP *are left downstage.* ALBA, DOMINGO,
PARMA *and* LERMA *wait.*

INQUISITOR.
    I am in the presence of the King.

PHILIP.
    Eminence . . .
    You are.

INQUISITOR.

Why have you summoned me?

PHILIP.

Leave us.

The others go.

My soul is not at peace.
I have killed a man.

INQUISITOR.

Was it a murder you can justify?

PHILIP.

He was a traitor – a deceiver –

INQUISITOR.

The Marquis Posa.

PHILIP.

You knew?

INQUISITOR.

The Holy Office has known for many years
what you have taken a lifetime to discover.

PHILIP (*feeling betrayed*).

I had a traitor in my Court – you *knew*?

INQUISITOR.

The whole course of his life
is set down in the records of the Holy Office
from the moment of his birth to his death –
a moment ago.

PHILIP.

Yet you let him roam free?

INQUISITOR.

I did not. Wherever he went, I was with him.
He was hooked on an invisible line –
seeming to swim wherever he had a mind to go.
At any moment I could have reeled him in.

PHILIP.

If Your Eminence knew I had fallen into Posa's hands,
why did you not warn me?

INQUISITOR.

A more pertinent question is why did you not examine your
own conscience?

Why did you not pray for guidance?

I was watching as you threw yourself into his power –
eagerly – blindly . . .

Am I to believe you did not smell his treachery?

He stank of heresy! – and, as a heretic,

he was a property of the Holy Office.

What business had the Crown to filch our Marquis from us?

You ask why I did not warn you? You dare to question *me*!

Do not meddle, sir –

If you think to hoodwink me –

how shall I see into the souls I seek?

O you were at fault! – you set aside the fatherly care I have
of you,

and took the devil into your embrace.

If you can fawn upon one heretic

how can you justify the sacrifice of one hundred thousand
others?

PHILIP.

He too was sacrificed.

INQUISITOR.

No! He was murdered! Casually, secretly, vengefully.

His blood should have been shed to glorify our faith.

This man was mine! My prize! Nurtured, cherished many
years –

An eloquent heretic to be sacrificed to Truth –

I'd planned his death over his whole lifetime.

Who gave you authority, sir, to strike him down?

I can smell his blood still warm upon your hands.

PHILIP.

Forgive me.

INQUISITOR.

I have leaned against a crumbling wall.

Your iron rule – sixty years of unquestioning faith –

dissolve in an idle hour of girlish infatuation.

PHILIP.

I looked into his eyes.

INQUISITOR.

What did you see there?

His blind eyes look into PHILIP's.

Did the world look different reflected in those eyes?
Did poisonous minerals lose their power to hurt?
Did the truth of Holy Church seem lies?
Did good and evil join in redemption?
What was this man to you?

PHILIP.

I have never known affection.
To give nor to receive it.
I've never felt another soul
reach down and touch my own.
I've never . . .

INQUISITOR.

Men – souls – are numbers – no more than that.
There's no need to distinguish one from another.
To do so is to grow weak! – Numbers. Mere numbers!
Put more iron in your soul, King!
A ruler must be strong – remote – aloof.
Or do you crave equality with your subjects?
No! What claim has equality to a crown?

PHILIP.

I'm one man – just a poor, frail remnant of humanity.
We are all weak – we must all fail.
You ask too much of me.

INQUISITOR.

I demand everything of you – too much, and more –
In the name of Him who gave you everything. Everything!
You cannot free yourself of His control.
He holds you on a golden leash – a collar of gold about
your neck.
You're His slave – at His beck and call –
or you are no king – nothing.

I stand before you now,
but I tell you, King, had you not summoned me,
tomorrow I would have summoned you to stand before me.

PHILIP *kneels submissively and kisses the* INQUISITOR*'s*
ring.

Now tell me why you brought me here.
I would not willingly subject myself
to such another trial of your faith.

PHILIP.
My son is plotting treason.

INQUISITOR.
Then your course is clear.

PHILIP.
It must be all or nothing.

INQUISITOR.
'Nothing' is to let a traitor go free. What is 'all'?

PHILIP.
His death.

INQUISITOR.
Ask your question.

PHILIP.
How may our faith allow
a father to kill his son?

INQUISITOR.
To save the world from sin
God the Father looked down and wept
as his son was nailed upon the cross.

PHILIP.
Men set him there.
What man would not condemn my act?

INQUISITOR.
A man who has faith.
A man who accepts God has a higher purpose.

PHILIP.

My own nature will cry out against the act!
Should faith silence a man's conscience?

INQUISITOR.

Nature without faith is itself unnatural.
Your faith *must* silence those inner voices.

PHILIP.

If I resign to your judgement
will that free me of the deed?

INQUISITOR.

It will.

PHILIP.

If I condemn my only son to death,
for whom then was my work on earth?

INQUISITOR.

For desolation!
Better the death of a prince
than an empire full of loose souls.

Come.

PHILIP.

Where?

INQUISITOR.

This child will lead the way.

Two more DOMINICANS *drag in the* PAGE. *His body is broken and bloody, and he has been talking.*

Scene Twenty

QUEEN ELIZABETH's *private chapel. Dark. Candles burning on the altar.* ELIZABETH *kneels in prayer, saying the rosary. A* DOMINICAN MONK *comes in through a secret door hidden by a holy image and genuflects to the image of*

Christ on the altar. He goes and stands behind ELIZABETH.
It is, of course, CARLOS. *He takes off the habit, revealing that
he is in half armour – ready for travel – looking heroic.*

CARLOS.
Elizabeth.

ELIZABETH.
In coming here, you're risking everything.

CARLOS.
No – we're quite safe.

ELIZABETH.
I can't see you in the darkness. My eyes are filling with
tears –

He kisses her hands almost in tears himself.

We mustn't weep – we mustn't –
tears are not enough to weep what we've lost.
I swore to Rodrigo I'd keep you strong.

CARLOS *(embracing her)*.
Oh, I am strong – so strong –
I shall perform miracles in his name
and dedicate my victories to his memory –

ELIZABETH.
I promised him I'd never abandon you . . .
And – why should I fear to say it? – there can be no sin
between us –
I swore to confess my love for you.

CARLOS.
Elizabeth –

ELIZABETH.
To love you unchangingly – and forever –
to obey the impulse of my heart.

CARLOS *(takes her hand)*.
That's good – never fear to love me.
God's blessing is upon us.
It always was.

We're sure of it.
We've needed no mumbled marriage vows –
no bankrupt ceremony – the nod of Church and State.
We have always loved and our hearts have kept our vows.

ELIZABETH.
I've kept hidden in my heart
this parting gift of truth.

CARLOS.
Now I receive it from your lips.

He kisses her.

I've been a dreamer too long.
Now I shall act.
We'll be apart.
How shall we sustain each other?
Somehow – somehow we must find a way.
I cannot fail – I must not fail him –
I promise you – with your love and the memory of his –
I'm equal to the task.

ELIZABETH.
You will not fail, Carlos.

CARLOS.
We've so little time.
My horses are waiting – friends –
They'll take me to Cadiz – from there I sail to Vlissingen –
Pray for me, I . . .
I need a lifetime to say what I came to say
and suddenly there's no time at all.

ELIZABETH.
We'll have the time to come.
God go with you.
Travel safely, travel swiftly.

I said I wouldn't weep. (*She is doing.*)
I have such faith in you, Carlos,
Such faith –

CARLOS.
> I shall return with victory.
> When you see me in Madrid again
> I'll be welcomed as Spain's king –

ELIZABETH.
> The whole world will welcome you –
> I will welcome you.

CARLOS.
> Bid me farewell – one last time –

> *He kisses her.*

> I hold you in my arms.
> The stars smile down upon us –
> Fortune will favour us –
> I hold you in my arms.
> Nothing can ever part us –

ELIZABETH (*giving packages and money*).
> You must go – quickly – take these.

> KING PHILIP *appears in the darkness of the chapel,*
> *unnoticed by* CARLOS *and* ELIZABETH.

CARLOS.
> I'll write to you when I reach Ghent –
> Then everything will be in the open –
> I'll negotiate with the King on equal terms at last –
> man to man – no more secrets – no more deception –

> *Putting on the monk's habit.*

> And I'll no longer call him father.
> We'll be free of each other –
> Nature's already dead in him –
> He no longer has a son.

PHILIP.
> No more deception.
> He no longer has a son.

> ELIZABETH *collapses in* CARLOS' *arms. Out of the*
> *darkness come the* PAGE, *the* GRAND INQUISITOR,

MONKS *carrying flaming torches and instruments of torture, and* SOLDIERS.

CARLOS.
Elizabeth! – O God!

PHILIP.
Cardinal. I've played my part.
Now you must play yours.

End.